"NOT MY DAUGHTER"

Facing Up to Adolescent Pregnancy

Other Books by the Author

Population and Family Planning: Analytical Abstracts for Social Work Educators and Related Disciplines, Katherine Brownell Oettinger and Jeffrey D. Stansbury, International Association of Schools of Social Work. (1972)

Social Work in Action: An International Perspective on Population and Family Planning, Katherine Brownell Oettinger, International Association of Schools of Social Work. (1975)

"NOT MY DAUGHTER"

Facing Up to Adolescent Pregnancy

Katherine B. Oettinger

with Elizabeth C. Mooney

Prentice-Hall, Inc., Englewood Cliffs, New Jersey

All names used in the case histories cited in this book are fictitious.

"Not My Daughter": Facing Up to Adolescent Pregnancy
by Katherine B. Oettinger with Elizabeth C. Mooney
Copyright © 1979 by Katherine B. Oettinger
All rights reserved. No part of this book may be reproduced in any form ·or by
any means, except for the inclusion of brief quotations in a review, without
permission in writing from the publisher.
Printed in the United States of America
Prentice-Hall International, Inc., London/Prentice-Hall of Australia, Pty.
Ltd., Sydney/Prentice-Hall of Canada, Ltd., Toronto/Prentice-Hall of India
Private Ltd., New Delhi/Prentice-Hall of Japan, Inc., Tokyo/Prentice-Hall of
Southeast Asia Pte. Ltd., Singapore/Whitehall Books Limited, Wellington,
New Zealand

10 9 8 7 6 5 4 3 2 1

Library of Congress Cataloging in Publication Data

Oettinger, Katherine Brownell.
  Not my daughter.

  Includes index.
  1. Adolescent mothers—United States. 2. Youth—United States—
Sexual behavior. 3. Pregnancy, Adolescent—United States. I. Mooney,
Elizabeth Comstock. II. Title.
HQ759.4.032   362.8'3   79-13330
ISBN 0-13-623850-5

Acknowledgments

Many skilled hands participated in the making of this book. I would especially like to thank Takey Crist, M.D., F.A.C.O.G., F.A.C.S., Director of the Crist Clinic for Women in Jacksonville, North Carolina, Clinical Professor, University of North Carolina School of Medicine, and recipient of numerous awards and honors in the field of obstetrics and gynecology, who was responsible for writing all the medical and factual data supplied for Chapter 7, "The Abortion Option." His additional contributions throughout the book include not only technical knowledge but a compassionate understanding of human factors. The three days I spent visiting the Crist Clinic, where over 1,200 teenagers come yearly for comprehensive medical care, provided me with valuable insight into the broad spectrum of feelings surrounding the decision to terminate an unwanted pregnancy.

I would like as well to thank Mary Lee Tatum, M.Ed., certified as a counselor by the American Association of Sex Educators, Counselors and Therapists, for sharing her knowledge, gained from daily experience with today's junior-high and high-school students at George Mason High School in Falls Church, Virginia. As well as giving support to the purpose of this book, she enlivened it with vignettes from real life. Her work demonstrates the value of up-to-date methods of teaching decision making in relation to reproductive behavior. I benefited greatly from her fresh, realistic approach and her understanding of parents and community relations.

J. Stephen Kirkpatrick, Ph.D., Director of Education at Planned Parenthood of Southern Arizona, also deserves special mention. He provided insights into the problems of a wide variety of teens from different socio-economic and ethnic groups, and enriched the book by sharing with me their answers to questionnaires exploring their knowledge of sex. His perceptive review of the preliminary version of the book inspired helpful additions to the text.

I am grateful as well to Harriet Pilpel, a partner in Greenbaum, Wolff & Ernst of New York, longtime general counsel to Planned Parenthood Federation of America, and a leading advocate for the rights of adolescents. She gave generously of her valuable time to review those portions of the book dealing with legal issues.

My long years of association with Mary Calderone, M.D., M.P.H., president of the Sex Information and Education Society of the United States, Inc., and a creative pioneer in the field of human sexuality, have left their stamp on this book. I wish to express my appreciation here for her seasoned judgment, which has provided perspective on various of its concepts.

Margaret Hickey, J.D., public affairs editor of *Ladies' Home Journal,* former president of the National Federation of Business and Professional Women's Clubs, for many years consultant in various capacities with Department of State and public and voluntary organizations, reviewed portions of this book and used her skill with the blue pencil. I am grateful for her distinguished assistance.

Both the following gave valuable assistance by reviewing the statistical and factual aspects of this book: Arthur Campbell, deputy director, the Behavioral Science Branch, National Institutes of Health, Public Health Service, DHEW; and Catherine S. Chilman, Ph.D., School of Social Welfare, University of Wisconsin, author of the landmark text *Adolescent Sexuality in a Changing American Society: Social and Psychological Perspectives,* an HEW publication.

Special thanks are also due to Susan Ross, director of the New York based Youth Values Project. Theories about teenage values, attitudes, and motivation which formerly depended on speculation have been documented by her work with teenage consultants. Her study is drawn upon at many appropriate points in this book.

Michael Hirsh, an executive producer and documentary producer at WTTW/Chicago Public Television, generously shared with me tapes he made of adolescent clinical discussion groups. His skillful leadership of rap sessions with teenagers seeking contraceptive advice resulted in documentation which adds greatly to the immediacy of the text.

I am grateful for the assistance of Dorothy Bradbury, former director of the Division of Publications of the Children's Bureau, for her assistance with the Introduction, "A Look Back—A Look Forward." She contributed not only useful historical information but her characteristic enthusiasm and insight into changing trends.

Additional thanks are due to the host of colleagues in leadership positions in active agencies who gave generous interviews and provided up-to-date information. Among those frequently consulted were Phillip Sarrel, M.D., of the Yale University Health Services; Lulu Mae Nix, Ed.D., Director, Office of Adolescent Pregnancy Programs, Department of Health, Education and Welfare; Leni Wildflower, M.P.H., Youth Advocacy Programs, Southern California; William Ryerson, M. Phil., Director of Youth and Student Affairs Division, The Population Institute, Washington, D.C.; Gary Goldsmith, M.D., Medical Director, The Door, New York City; Patricia Schiller, M.A., J.D., Executive Director, Founder of the American Association of Sex Educators, Counselors and Therapists; Joan Morgenthau, M.D., Medical Director of Mount Sinai Adolescent Health Center and Professor of Clinical Pediatrics, Mount Sinai School of Medicine, New York City; Louise Peloquin, M.S.W., Counselor, Planned Parenthood of Metropolitan Washington; Ralph Gause, M.D., Health Department, Mississippi; Marion Howard, Ph.D., Clinical Director of Teen Services Program, Grady Memorial Hospital, Emory University, and Assistant Professor, department of gyn/obs; Reginald Lourie, M.D., psychiatrist and research scientist at Mental Health Study Center and Professional Associates Child and Adolescent Services, Washington, D.C.; and Joan Harriman, M.Ed., Executive Director, Catholic Alternatives, New York City.

I am indebted to Judith Jacobsen, who served as editorial secretary between her studies for the Virginia bar examination. During our too brief association, she brought precision and organizational skills to this work, particularly in the assembling of the appendix.

Finally, my deepest appreciation goes to my editor, Mariana Fitzpatrick, for her extraordinary helpfulness in encouraging me to begin this book and sustaining me to the end.

Introduction

A Look Back— A Look Forward

My concern for the adolescent pregnant girl goes back many years. As a young psychiatric social worker, I worked with immigrant families whose breadwinners were either unemployed or working for low wages in the Pennsylvania anthracite mines during the Depression.

One cold day in January, as a visiting nurse and I were leaving a needy household, a woman on the porch of a neighboring house beckoned frantically. When we entered her clean but primitive house, we found a young girl lying in a blood-soaked bed.

The mother explained the situation by saying, "I told Mary to leave them boys alone." Quite evidently she had been working with the girl to induce an abortion.

When the nurse called a doctor, he said exasperatedly, "I told those people that when they do this sort of thing they should call the undertaker, not me."

Despite the mother's protest, the nurse called the emergency room in a nearby hospital for an ambulance. Even with skilled staff trained to meet such crises, Mary died a few hours later. She was sixteen.

How and when, I asked myself, would we find ways to prevent, treat and assist such young pregnant girls? Why could this family not have found help?

The answer was obvious. In this community, as in most others, appropriate services simply did not exist. The stigma of pregnancy outside of marriage was so strong that Mary and her mother had seen no way out except through the induced abortion that led to the death of the young girl and her baby. This early encounter remains engraved on my memory, urging me to help prevent such unwanted pregnancies and their consequences.

Opportunities to do so have come in many forms. I have had the great privilege of working with many likeminded professional groups on problems confronting young parents, their unplanned babies, and their bewildered families. As a nation we have come far—but not far enough—in the years since my first haunting experience.

I met many young women like Mary in the ensuing years, so when I was asked in the late 1940s to administer the new community mental health program of the Pennsylvania Department of Welfare and to develop studies on community organization at the University of Pittsburgh, I welcomed a chance to act.

In Pennsylvania, as in most states, pregnant adolescents were routinely being put out of school on the grounds that they were a bad influence on their peers. Concerned by this situation, I worked with mental health centers throughout the state to obtain services for these school-aged girls. As a result of combined efforts, in cooperation with the Department of Education, visiting teachers were assigned to tutor homebound children under the Division of Handicapped Children. Clearly, pregnant teenagers were neither "homebound" nor "handicapped," but accepting help under this category of the educational system seemed the only possible compromise at the time to secure a learning program for the pregnant girl.

When, in the early fifties, I served as Dean of the School of Social Work at Boston University, I saw the problem of teenage pregnancy from another perspective —the training of social workers. At that time, means of preventing pregnancy was a subject virtually untouched in the classroom. As a way of increasing student awareness, I initiated a university field work program during my term as dean. It offered students a direct opportunity to participate in health and welfare activities, sensitizing future professionals to the needs of unmarried mothers.

In 1957, President Dwight D. Eisenhower appointed me chief of the Children's Bureau for the Department of Health, Education and Welfare (HEW), a position I held for over ten years. This gave me a unique chance to act on the national level, directly through state health and welfare departments. Once again my thoughts turned to the unmarried adolescent girl. During this period, facilities for helping unwed mothers were few and far between. Many young mothers abandoned their babies, often leaving them in hospitals which were not geared for rearing a well baby. Social workers struggled to keep nurseries from becoming overcrowded with homeless infants.

Welfare agencies had few and inadequate services, chiefly focused on helping the mother make a decision on keeping or releasing her child for adoption, with little or no help offered to the mother wishing to keep her baby. She could turn to the Salvation Army or a Florence Crittenton Home where the emphasis was on residential care, with protection of anonymity and recovery from childbirth the main focuses.

I felt strongly that an unintended pregnancy should not change the whole scenario of a girl's life. She should be helped to live up to her highest potential—and there was no hope at all of her achieving this if she was viewed as a social outcast. It seemed to me that here was an important priority which we at the Children's Bureau, with all our varied programs dealing with maternal and child health, crippled children, child welfare, and juvenile delinquency programs, could meet by coordinating services to pregnant adolescents.

Beginning in 1962, the Bureau made an important breakthrough by allocating child-welfare action research funds for a demonstration project at the Webster School in Washington, D.C., a special education facility for girls containing units for elementary and high-school age, in an effort to show that comprehensive services could be given pregnant adolescents in a public-school setting.

Gradually such programs spread to other schools, changed to a policy of keeping these students in their regular classes, and eventually led to the elimination of all restrictions on educational opportunities for the pregnant girl. Today, under the auspices of a voluntary organization, The National Alliance Concerned with School-Age Parents, which grew out of the initial pilot effort, this program renders progressive services through affiliates all over the country.

In 1965, new provisions of the Social Security Act

made maternal and child health funds administered by the Children's Bureau available to provide adolescents with comprehensive health services, including sex education and family planning information. The Bureau was in a key position to take another important step in providing family planning services as an integral part of its grants to state maternal and child health programs. Before this period, adolescents were shortchanged because most public health clinics would provide contraception only if a woman already had at least one child. The congressional appropriation committee designated one sixth of these state maternal and child health grants-in-aid to family planning services. The Children's Bureau administrative policy made clear that all individuals be given free access to these contraceptive services regardless of age or marital status.

More significant legislation for family planning came later, in 1967, expanding and strengthening the Children's Bureau's health and welfare programs for mothers and children. States were required to offer family planning services to all appropriate recipients of welfare assistance. In subsequent years family planning activities were incorporated into many other health and social programs granted federal funding.

During these expansive times there were stirrings within HEW that culminated in Secretary John Gardner's announcing departmental priority for family planning programs. In 1968, he established a new post of Deputy Assistant Secretary for Population and Family Planning and asked me to serve in this capacity.

Here was my chance. On behalf of HEW, I immediately called together a group of twenty prominent physicians, lawyers, educators, and social workers to discuss problems related to teenage pregnancy. Everyone in this professional group had had firsthand experience in dealing with adolescents who became parents while still children themselves.

These experts recognized the complex problems involved in dealing with teenage pregnancy: the medical risks; the legal questions; the social and educational hazards; the supportive services necessary; and the public attitudes that made specific action difficult. Despite the difficulties, the experts agreed without reservation that teenage contraceptive programs were a prime necessity if the physical, social, and educational well-being of these young people were to be preserved.

I became acutely aware as Deputy Assistant Secretary for Population and Family Planning, that problems of teenage pregnancy were not limited to the United States. As head of the U.S. delegation to the First Inter-American Congress on Population and Family Planning, held in Caracas, Venezuela, under the auspices of the Pan-American Health Organization, I found that the discussions of sex education and contraception had a familiar ring. Earlier, I had heard the same issues debated in maternal and child health settings when I visited less developed countries as U.S. delegate to the Executive Board of UNICEF. More and more, through such experiences and subsequent liaison work with the State Department, I grew to realize that family planning was an international problem.

When, in 1971, upon leaving government service, I became consultant to the Council on Social Work Education to organize and coordinate the first conference dealing with social work responsibility for family planning on the international level, I was able to act on this growing concern. Funded by a grant from the Agency for International Development (AID), we invited over one hundred delegates from all over the world to come to the East-West Center in Honolulu, Hawaii, to explore how and where the social work profession could undertake its role in this emerging field.

For the next seven years I was to pursue my activities on the international level. In the early seventies I was named Chief Consultant for an AID-supported project of the International Association of Schools for Social Work. The project aimed to develop qualified personnel for participation in all family planning activities, including adolescents' needs, and required consultation visits to schools of social work in the Middle East and Asia.

In 1976, I served as the Coordinator for the Inter-hemispheric Conference on Adolescent Fertility sponsored by AID and six international organizations. One hundred and sixty opinion-makers and professional leaders from thirty-nine nations attended this conference and their recommendations were included in the proceedings which have had worldwide distribution. As Director of Adolescent Studies of the Inter-American Dialogue Center I went on to help develop further AID-supported dialogues in Latin American and Caribbean countries.

The necessity for such action aimed at meeting individual nations' needs was clearly great. *In 1975, close to 13 million girls worldwide became mothers before becoming adults.*

A lifetime of experience in the field has gone into the making of this book. For me, and for many of the other determined people dedicated to helping young adolescent parents, the way has been long, often discouraging, and sometimes frustrating. About one thing, however, we remain certain: the problems of unmarried adolescent parents are not going to fade away quietly by themselves.

The number of unmarried mothers under 16 in the United States has increased 90 percent since 1960. Adolescents give birth to more than half of all babies born out of wedlock. We cannot afford the ostrich-like view expressed by one state senator when I was conferring with him a few years ago. "We don't have any urgent problems with teenage pregnancy in our state," he said with some satisfaction. It wasn't true then. It isn't true now. Every state and every community confronts these problems, and they must be faced.

Adolescent pregnancies carry too heavy a penalty to be ignored—for the teenagers involved, for their families, the community, and for our nation as a whole.

An effective program to combat teenage pregnancy requires input at many levels. It is essential to provide the legal and social atmosphere in which programs for young people have a chance of succeeding; hence the need for strong government support. Voluntary agencies emphasizing prevention to teenagers, and offering help when prevention has come too late, must act in urban and rural areas. Local community activity plus needed federal-state support should provide alternatives so that young people can make informed choices regarding their sexual behavior. Teachers, clergy, social workers, medical aides, volunteers, and others who touch the lives of today's youth can open discussions of matters once considered unfit to mention. I hope this book may help them in their task.

Parents, however, remain the basic sex educators, so it is primarily to them that I address this book. I hope as well that the new generation will find in these pages an accurate reflection of their thoughts and feelings about their sexuality.

Contents

Acknowledgments   v

Introduction: A Look Back—A Look Forward   xi

1   Teenagers Speak   1

2   Facing Facts   9

3   Building Healthy Sexuality in the Home *Prevention*   21

4   Breaking the Silence Barrier   43

5   Behind the Male Myth   57

6   It Happened: Decisions, Decisions   67

7   The Abortion Option   81

8   Planning for the Baby   97

9   Working for Community Change   113

10 Peer Counseling: Why and How   133

11 Innovative Programs Tailored to Teens   145

12 Examining Values: The Essential Ingredient   157

Resource Guide   163

Index   181

To my sons,
Malcolm and John, who have given
lifelong encouragement
to a working mother

1

Teenagers Speak

"It's not like I'm really promiscuous," she says. The tremble in her voice is scarcely noticeable. "It just sounds that way. I only sleep with one person."

The gynecologist, a specialist in adolescent sexuality, nods.

"When you're doing it, it just seems so right and natural. But I'm so scared. I never thought I'd be doing this. I feel so guilty. We both do."

"Have you been using any contraceptive?"

She pushes back her long hair.

"I don't know if I'd feel right taking those things. You shouldn't use them if you're not married."

The doctor writes. He has heard it all before, thousands of times.

"You've been very lucky," he says mildly. She nods.

"The way I see it, if I use birth control, that makes me a bad girl. If I don't use anything, even if I get pregnant, I'm a good girl who got caught."

Although she's not pregnant this time, she's terrified that she will be and is seeking advice. She's in love for the first time, and having regular sex. Since both she and her partner believe that birth control is "for when you're married," she has already lived through at least two late periods, the special hell reserved for those young girls who, whether from ignorance or confusion, have not been using contraception.

"If only we were older. Then we'd get married. But we're still both so young. Besides, I couldn't be treasurer of my high-school sorority if I was married."

This girl has many sisters—11 million of them all across the country—each with her own story: carefully reared or neglected, children of the affluent or the poor, the educated and the school dropout, the talented and the retarded. They seem wise beyond their years, but they are also abysmally ignorant, at once tough and vulnerable, a restless generation, many without real goals, direction, or aspirations. In their search for easy satisfaction and their failure to establish their own values, their unprotected sexual activity has brought America into a prominent fifth place among Western nations in incidence of pregnancy during the teen years.

Another girl now sits facing the gynecologist.

"How many different people have you had intercourse with?" he asks.

It takes her a while to count up.

"Six in the past ten months. You think I'm weird, I bet."

The doctor shakes his head. Nothing surprises him.

"Ever had oral intercourse?"

She nods, twisting a strand of hair. The small room is quiet as the doctor writes.

The silence weighs on the girl. She shifts in her chair, pushing up her sleeves. She is conventionally pretty, dressed in the uniform of her generation: the ubiquitous jeans, clodhopper shoes, too-large shirt.

"I feel really mixed up," she says, and now there is less bravado in her voice. "I almost feel like sex is expected of me. My attitude toward sex has become really warped. Sometimes the way I act scares me."

The doctor continues to write.

"What I really want is somebody who loves me so much that he doesn't want anyone else. I really want to get married and have babies."

She is seventeen and has venereal disease. She had an abortion two years ago and has been sexually active and on pills ever since.

By today's standards, she's old. Girls barely into their teens are now often sexually experienced.

"Sex is a natural thing and it's—I don't see anything wrong with it," says the 14-year-old in the chair.

"How long have you been sleeping with your boyfriend?" the doctor asks.

"About a year."

Twenty out of every 100 girls are sexually active by the time they are fifteen years old, according to a study by the Alan Guttmacher Institute. By eighteen, 43 of the 100 have had intercourse, and by nineteen, half. Voices like the above are not those of a select few. Their words, released from tapes made in a gynecologist's office, echo the experiences of their sisters everywhere. Consider for a moment a rap session conducted by award-winning TV documentary producer Michael Hirsh, working on an article for parents entitled "What Your Teenage Daughter Wants to Tell You About Sex":

Twenty girls, ranging in age from just 15 to 19 are scattered around the small conference room, bare except for the oversized throw pillows on the floor. They are waiting their turn to see the Planned Parenthood gynecologist at the weekly Teen Scene session in Chicago's Loop. While they wait, we [TV narrator and group] talk.

"How many of you have had sex in your own home?"

Laughter. 18 hands go up.

"How many in your boyfriend's home?" More laughter. 16 hands.

"Where else do you have sex? In cars?"

A chorus of "no's" and "once in a while's."

'Where else?"

'In motels," say a 15-year-old, two 16-year-olds, and a 17-year-old.

"When you're 15?"

"I went to one with my boyfriend when I was 14," says the button-nosed blonde who looks as if she could still get into the movies for half-price.

✕   *"When do girls start having sex?" I inquire. Bursts of laughter.*

"At 12?" More laughter.

One inner-city girl says, "Some do."

"13?" Giggles.

"I just started half a year ago," volunteers an almost 17-year-old suburban girl.

Now several of the group agree on an answer.

✕   *"Right in high school. At the beginning. In your freshman year, that's when it happens most often. But some start in eighth grade."*

"Do you think virginity is a thing of the past?" asks the reporter for WEPR in Clemson, South Carolina, of a fourteen-year-old on a program dealing with adolescence.

"Yeah."

✳ Despite their apparent sophistication, adolescents today are the ultimate conformists, highly sensitive to peer pressure. Their stumbling words on Hot Lines and in doctors' offices show a frightening lack of comprehension of how they arrived at the trouble in which they so often find themselves.

"Everybody was doing it. I didn't particularly care for it [intercourse] at first," says the cool young voice on a tape. "You just do it, you don't think about it."

✗ "It's not that you're in love at my age," says the 13-year-old interviewed for a national public radio program on American adolescence. "It's just something that, I don't know, it just *happens*. I guess partly 'cause everybody else does it. If no one else in the whole school was doing it, I don't think I would either. I guess it's just something you do. It's sort of social pressure."

"I thought you had to *plan* a family," says the young boy sitting in the sex counselor's office beside the young girl who is tightly clutching his hand.

✗ "Wendy and I never thought you could have a baby unless you mean to. We never did it with anyone else."

The constant in the chorus of voices is the fear that parents will discover what is going on. Cool or terrified, they speak as one when it comes to their fathers and mothers.

"Tell my parents?" they say in almost identical words. "Are you kidding? I can't tell my parents. There's *no way* I can tell them."

"The worst part is my mother," says the pregnant

young girl. "I can't let her find out. She's religious, and I mean religious. The very first thing she would do is talk to her minister. And I know he'd insist I get married. That's what he used on my sister's best friend—she was 16 and her boyfriend was 30. And after the wedding it turned out that she wasn't even pregnant. They're miserable.

"Anyway, I can't hurt her that way. I could stand her getting mad—then it might be all over. But she would just suffer inside. When I think about everything she's done for us . . . She couldn't stand the news. I just keep asking myself why I ever let it happen."

Michael Hirsh's tapes confirm this fear of confiding in parents:

"Do your mothers know you're down here?" I [Hirsh] asked the girls.

"No. And if she did, I'd be hanged from the ceiling," one answered.

"How about you? What would your mom say?"

"I'm not sure," the black 17-year-old replies. "My mother always tells me to come to her and talk about these things, but when I try . . ." her voice trails off. She thinks for a moment, then says firmly, "I think her ideas and opinions are so set that she's not going to listen and really try to understand my point of view. Of course I might be surprised . . ."

"She doesn't know I'm here," says another. Then she pauses. "She must know . . . but she won't talk about it." There is no doubt from the tone in her voice that she longs to talk over things with her mother but knows that all she will get is a lecture.

Many fear discussion with their parents because it can touch off reprisals. Hirsh's rap session continues:

"If my mom knew I was coming down here," says a girl, "she'd start watching me real carefully. That's what happened when I just started talking about sex. She made me be in by ten o'clock for a couple of weeks."

There is abundant evidence that adolescents are judging parental reaction correctly. In a pilot program designed to provide continuing education for pregnant teens, it was found that most of their mothers had not spoken to their daughters about sex until they suspected that they were pregnant. A few gave earlier dark warnings. "Keep your skirts down," said Margie's mother as her daughter left on a date. Another girl's mother cautioned her more gently, "Don't sit out in the car too long."

"If someone tells you not to do something, that's just what you're doing to do," says Margie, "even though it's not all that great and some boys just use you."

Occasionally mothers see disaster coming and try to avoid it.

"Mom told me about birth control," says the well-developed 13-year-old who looks twice her age. "She wanted me to get an IUD. But the older girls weren't doing it and I wanted to do like them. Now I'm pregnant. I've failed my mother. I don't know what to say to her."

Left to make their decisions alone, some teenagers resort to the comforting support of liquor or drugs.

"Help me to understand about drugs," says the sex counselor to the freshman who has contracted a vaginal infection after sexual relations with several partners.

"Sex is more intense under drugs," she replies. "You're not so aware of the other person."

"Where do you get drugs?"

There is a tiny pause, and then she laughs.

"It's everywhere. You can trip on the street, or at

your friend's house. It's like buying a candy bar. Half of the senior class in my high school is on drugs."

Where do they go for help? Where do they get their sex education?

"Off the bathroom walls or from the guys at school," says the young man who is afraid he will make his girl pregnant.

What have they learned from their torment and mistakes? How will they teach their own children?

"I plan to be honest and not just tell them the mechanics," says a 17-year-old girl. "Kids need to know the same things that grownups do about sex, their choices, their responsibilities. I want my daughter to know *everything*."

Voices like Margie's and the others cry out to be heard. They call to us everywhere, throughout the nation. What can parents and concerned community workers do to help?

First of all, painful as it may be, we must listen.

2

Facing Facts

The June 1958 issue of *Newsweek* magazine contained the following quote: "The sharp rise in the number of young unwed mothers in the U.S. is one of our most tragic and disturbing problems."

This quote comes from my first news conference as the newly appointed chief of the Children's Bureau in HEW when I was asked what I considered the nation's most urgent social and health issues.

What appeared over 20 years ago as a threat has escalated into a full-fledged disaster that is rapidly making its mark on America. News commentators are calling it an epidemic, a word previously reserved for disease. Nationwide, nearly 1 in 5 women who give birth each year is an adolescent. The teenage birth rate in the United States is among the highest in the world for developed countries.

One out of four babies born in our nation's capital in 1978 had a teenage mother.

It is natural to want to ignore such distressing facts and figures. Michael Hirsh confesses that while making his TV film he was forced to leave the room on one occasion, due to his discomfort at the explicitness of the teenagers' rapping. He probably speaks for most of us when he remarks: "We have mixed feelings about whether we *really* want to know what our kids are doing."

That parents do fail to face up to teenage pregnancy has been given credence by Dr. Greer Litton Fox in her study reported in 1979 at the Merrill Palmer Institute in Detroit. Separate interviews with a representative sample of 450 mothers and their 14- and 15-year-old daughters reveal that there is a wide gap between a mother's perception of her daughter's sex activity and the true nature of the young girl's behavior. To the question, "Do you think your daughter has had sexual intercourse?" only 10 percent of mothers interviewed answered yes. One third of their daughters answered yes to the same question. Ten percent of the sexually experienced girls said they had apprised their mothers of the true situation while 60 percent believed their mothers suspected, but did not discuss the matter. Here is clear evidence of an ostrichlike parental response.

The Fox study also noted that a larger percentage of girls whose mothers had talked to them about birth control remained virgins than those whose mothers' had not. The mothers' communication of their values and attitudes about contraception prior to any sexual intercourse proved more important to their daughters than the actual information provided.

With more than 1 million girls between the ages of 15 and 19 becoming pregnant each year in the United States, America's parents can no longer turn their heads.

Not all of these adolescents become mothers, of course. About 600,000 do, but over 300,000 terminate their pregnancies by abortion. This represents one third of all abortions performed in the United States. The rest experience involuntary pregnancy termination.

Particularly alarming is the fact that since 1960, adolescent mothers have been getting younger. This is partly due to biology as well as the changing sexual mores. Puberty arrives earlier for children today than it did a generation ago. Studies show that menses appear earlier with the passage of each generation. In 1870, the average age of first menstruation was about 17 in the Western world. Today it is 12.8 in the United States.

The trend toward too-early motherhood cuts through all socio-economic groups. The pregnancy rate is increasing among white girls in the 9 to 15 age group, according to Janet Forbush, director of National Alliance Concerned with School-Age Parents. In 1975, 86 percent more births to mothers under 15 appeared in the registration figures than in 1960—a total of 30,000 pregnancies, resulting in 13,000 births. Between 1966 and 1975, birth rates for white girls in this younger age group rose by 57 percent while birth rates for other adolescents of the same age group rose only 8 percent. Young non-white girls still bear five times as many babies as white girls, but ten years ago the rate was seven times as great.

Another chilling statistic, derived from a study by the National Center for Health Statistics, reveals that illegitimacy has soared by nearly 40 percent among teenagers—from 17 to 24 births per thousand in the past decade. The upward trend is again greater for whites than for non-whites.

Why, I am frequently asked, with birth control methods so improved, are we seeing such dramatic increases in teenage pregnancy, especially at a time when childbearing and illegitimacy among older women is on the decline? Are young people using the reliable contraceptives now available? Why, although sex education is gaining acceptance, does the rate of teenage pregnancy out of wedlock continue to climb? Social demographers have come up with no precise answers.

Current theories, bolstered by teenagers' own words, give the following clues to these puzzles. For one thing, an unexpectedly large number of teenagers are misinformed about how to use contraceptives or resent the "hassle" too often involved in procuring them. For another, many feel that contraception takes the romance out of sex. Then there is the fact that a surprising number of girls actually *want* to get pregnant. These attitudes reflect a mixture of innocence, ignorance, fatalism, and apathy. A Virginia gynecologist-psychiatrist claims that many of the pregnancies he sees are a deliberate form of rebellion.

"I thought my father wouldn't beat me anymore if I got pregnant," says one girl.

"My mother never loved me . . . I wanted somebody to be close to me," says another.

"I wanted to leave home," says a pregnant girl in the Louisiana Family Planning Program, "and I thought if I got pregnant my boyfriend would marry me."

"I don't want to think about it. It just happened," says a 15-year-old in a maternal and child health clinic in Mississippi.

Experts suggest yet another reason for the increasing incidence of teenage pregnancy: the fact that society no longer frowns so universally on childbirth out of wedlock. The tendency to mask premarital conception with a quick marriage has fallen from favor since 1971, when half of white marriages involved a pregnant bride. In 1976, only one third of white marriages took place because of premarital pregnancy.

A significant light shed on the baffling trend toward early parenthood comes from the findings of a Johns Hopkins national survey by Drs. Melvin Zelnik and John Kantner, professors in the School of Hygiene and Public Health. They conducted cross-sectional studies of the sexual experiences of female teenagers both in 1971 and 1976, reporting that the use of the most effective contraception among teenagers nearly doubled in the interval between their surveys. But the resulting benefit, an estimated prevention of 680,000 pregnancies each year, was all but eclipsed by two primary factors: the 30 percent increase in sexual intercourse among those studied in the later survey and the increase in proportion of that age group in the population. The stark fact remains that one out of ten adolescents is getting pregnant every year.

Only 27 percent of the women studied reported always using some form of contraception. Few know the time of greatest risk of conception during the menstrual cycle. Many believe that it is just before or after the period when it is actually in the middle of the cycle.

How many of the nation's adolescent women are at risk of unintended pregnancy? A nation-wide analysis of contraceptive services published in a special issue on Teenage Pregnancy, *Perspectives*, August 1978, reported that just over four million females aged 15 through 20 fall in this category. Of these at least 60 percent came from families earning well above the poverty level. The authors, Joy Dryfoos and Toni Heisler, both of whom were associated with The Alan Guttmacher Institute, estimate the number of sexually active girls aged 13 and 14 in danger of unwanted pregnancies at 375,000.

By the time young people graduate from high school today, half of them have been engaging in sexual intercourse; as might be expected, boys are more sexually active than girls. An ominous corollary to the sexual explosion is the alarming increase in venereal disease, which is currently appearing as a strain more difficult to diagnose and treat.

What all this adds up to is the frightening reality that thousands of adolescents who are slipping annually into sexual experimentation will not consistently use contraception or have no chance to get it. This does not mean, however, that they take sex lightly or casually. According to sex counselors, physicians, and others who deal with them, most frequently these young people feel they are in love and limit relationships to a single partner, although affairs may come and go.

One such young couple sought contraception advice at a referral clinic. The girl was not pregnant but worried constantly that she would be. "We've tried not to see each other," the boy told the counselor, "and we'll be all right for a while because we'll be apart at Christmas vacation. But I know it'll be the same thing when we come back, studying together, spending all that time alone. I know we'll have sex."

They hadn't been using contraceptives. The girl was worried about the pill's risk to her health and did not know of any other reliable method.

Could they tell her parents how they felt?

"I know what they'd say if they thought we were sleeping together," she said. "We've got to handle this on our own. That's why we're here for help."

Not *my* daughter, you say? Let me introduce you to Ellen.

Ellen was born pretty and bright into a family in a

high income bracket. The daughter of an attorney and a college-educated mother, she was given every educational opportunity. A model student, she worked hard and at sixteen won a coveted place in an experimental Russian-language program at a prominent West Coast university.

Here though, she was lonely. Competition among the gifted freshmen in the special project pushed her out of her accustomed first place. Perhaps if she threw herself into her love of riding, things would improve? She was soon dividing her time between the demanding school program and a nearby stable.

She met a young man there. They spent more and more time together and Ellen's first romance ended in pregnancy.

She dropped out of school, married the boy, and was divorced a year later. An infant is demanding under the best of circumstances; the aloneness of a single mother struggling to get ahead can make a baby a crushing burden. Ellen is still trying to pick up the pieces of her life. Her parents are heartbroken.

This young girl married her baby's father, but many others never do. Such marriages, when they occur, are often forced, arranged by distressed parents. "My mother says she and my father would drag 'that boy' to the church if they had to," says one girl receiving counseling at a maternal and child health clinic.

But parents shouldn't get all the blame for these marriages of convenience which so often fall apart. Today's child-mother-to-be often has a fuzzy, romantic dream of what the vows at the altar will do to her life. She may be unable or unwilling to see that the child she brings into the world may know its father only briefly and miss forever the stability of a caring and supportive home.

Divorce stalks marriages of girls 17 and under three times as often as those of young adults in their early 20s. The National Center statistical surveys show that over half of teenage marriages break up within five years.

What about the unmarried mother? What moves her to out-of-wedlock parenthood? One of her most often cited motivations is a longing for independence from a home where there is little understanding or love. The director of St. Anne's Home for Unwed Mothers in Los Angeles, an institution which houses ninety girls from 13 to 19 who are bringing their babies to term, says, "It is hard to understand the need for independence which could drive so many pregnant 15-year-olds to think they can support themselves and a baby on the $218 a month they can get from welfare in California." Fantasies of this kind are prevalent among teenagers, as are unreal notions of motherhood itself.

Although parents cannot think for their daughters, there are things they *can* do. They can make clear to them the *real-life perils* of pregnancy. If all parents were to lay before their daughters the actual specifics of what bringing another life into the world and caring for it involves, such honest communication could enormously affect young lives.

"The girl who has an illegitimate child at the age of 16 suddenly has 90 percent of her life's script written for her," says Arthur Campbell, research specialist at the National Institutes of Health, in a frequently quoted landmark report. ". . . Her life choices are few and most of them are bad." Whether she likes it or not, she is now a full-time baby-sitter. Studies also show that she will almost never catch up educationally with her peers. This is especially sad, since young pregnant girls are not always poor achievers, as is often believed. Many prematurely pregnant girls are above average in school grades.

The ability of the young mother to get and hold a job will be seriously hampered, and the younger she is, the poorer she is bound to be. She and her baby are probably destined to prolonged poverty. Money will almost certainly have to come from her parents or from public welfare assistance in the form of Aid to Families with Dependent Children. Not surprisingly, the father of the child is usually unable to help, since 75 percent of them are also in their teens. Half of the over $9 billion spent yearly on public welfare in the Aids to Families with Dependent Children program goes to families begun when the mother was a teenager.

Studies taken years after the first pregnancy show that early poverty patterns persist. Furthermore, among those teenage couples who marry, 20 years later they lag economically behind those who delayed marriage beyond the teen years.

Serious health hazards also threaten child mothers because their bodies are still growing and their endocrine systems are inadequately developed. If they are under 15, maternal death risks are 60 percent higher than for older girls. For the slightly older group from 16 to 19, the risk is 13 percent higher than for those who wait until their 20s to bear children. Under 19, mothers are more likely to miscarry, hemorrhage, or suffer toxemia in serious forms involving high blood pressure, seizures, and death. The risk is worse, as usual, under 15. Most of these potential mothers are slow to get vital prenatal care. Their diets are usually poor and they are under severe emotional stress.

If they deliver safely, they are still apt to suffer from postnatal anemia. "Very young women," says Charles Lowe, Special Assistant for Child Health Affairs, HEW, "are biologically too immature for effective childbearing." Growth of the adolescent mother may be stunted since the potential for optimum height is not reached until four to five years after first menses. The fusion of bones may not have been accomplished, especially in the very young pregnant girl.

The babies of too-young mothers enter a far more hostile world than those of older women. Adolescents, who are mothers of almost 1 out of 5 of all the babies born each year in this country, are responsible for 26 percent of those with low birth weight. Such infants tend to start life with developmental handicaps associated with such neurological ills as cerebral palsy, epilepsy, or mental retardation. Nobody is surprised to find that the babies of the youngest of the group are nearly 2½ times more likely than other newborns to suffer such complications which come with weights lower than five pounds. "Childhood mortality has been found to be 41 percent above the average for 1- to 4-year-old children born to adolescent mothers," reports Dr. Wendy Baldwin, social demographer at the National Institutes of Health.

Risks increase dramatically with the second and third child born to mothers during their teen years. To compound the grim picture, 1 out of 4 adolescents who had a child before the age of 18 is likely to have 3 more within 7 years. These children often live a neglected, abused life. Not infrequently the mother, pressed beyond endurance, simply walks out, leaving society to deal with the problems.

Children born out of wedlock are more than twice as likely to be physically abused than those of married couples, according to a large-scale study of such abuse by Georgia's Human Resources Department and the Atlanta-based National Center for Disease Control involving 2,000 cases of child abuse, including 26 deaths. Of the natural parents who abused their children, half were mothers—for the most part between 20 and 24 years old.

More than half of the abusing parents were teenagers when they bore their first child.

The cold statistics paint a frightening picture, but they cannot begin to measure the human suffering, loneliness, fear, boredom, discontent, and social disaster that swiftly follow the birth of an out-of-wedlock baby to an immature mother. Adolescence in this country is a period of delicate physical and psychological adjustments when the child becomes an adult in a crucial metamorphosis. Seven times more frequently than her contemporaries, a teenage mother gives up and attempts suicide. She sees no other way out.

What can we do to protect our sons and daughters from the ravages of too-early parenthood besides citing the damage it will cause to their lives? Perhaps our most important responsibility as parents and concerned citizens is to arm our young people to help themselves by giving them the information necessary to make intelligent choices.

I am well aware of the controversy over sex education and over making contraceptives available. Time and again I am asked whether I feel that freedom of information and access to birth control devices lead to promiscuous behavior. My reply given at the Population Tribunal held at the UN Population Conference at Bucharest in 1974 remains unchanged:

"Over the years I have developed the conviction that broader understanding of human sexuality, including the means of fertility control, can no longer be denied to adolescents, based on the false assumption that such information encourages promiscuity. It is becoming increasingly clear that young people will no longer tolerate twisted half-answers."

Proof that availability of contraceptives does not cause premarital intercourse among teenagers is evidenced by a 1977 report by The Urban and Rural Systems Associates. Results show that the typical adolescent who comes for family planning services has been sexually active for at least 6 months to more than one year *before* seeking contraceptives.

As concerned adults we must face the fact that young people today make their own sexual choices—choices which are not always responsible, as the statistics prove; choices which might have been unthinkable a generation ago. They are exposed to a much more stimulating and permissive sexual climate than their parents were. They, not their mothers and fathers, have ultimate control of their behavior. Parents who face this truth need to consider improving the quality of adolescent sexuality rather than futilely trying to eliminate its existence. The World Health Organization in a recent report offers a definition of what it terms "sexual health," which they suggest includes three basic elements:

> *a capacity to enjoy and control sexual and reproductive behavior in accordance with a social and personal ethic*

> *freedom from fear, shame, guilt, false beliefs, and other psychological factors inhibiting sexual response and impairing sexual relationships*

> *freedom from organic disorders, diseases, and deficiencies which interfere with sexual and reproductive functions*

I believe that respecting and fostering these concepts is part of a parent's job. Where this can be most effectively done is in the place where it all begins—the home.

3

Building Healthy Sexuality in the Home

"I have four young teenage daughters and I feel very afraid for them," wrote a mother to Phil Donahue, host of a Chicago-based syndicated talk show, who had devoted an entire program to the problems of communication about sexual matters between the generations. "I've tried to be open with them, but sometimes I can't reach them."

Donahue was snowed under by a blizzard of letters from parents in whom his show had touched a responsive chord. Again and again the letters reflected a style of upbringing in which sex was totally taboo as a subject between parent and child.

"When I started my period at 13, I had no idea what was going on," wrote a second listener. "Not another word was said about sex until I was 15 and became pregnant. Then my mother said, in a shocked tone of voice, 'You mean to tell me that you and Mike had intercourse?' "

"Like so many other parents of my generation [sex] was a subject which was in the closet," wrote another. "Our parents didn't talk much about it except to tell us it was wrong . . . Today . . . you can tell kids till you're blue in the face, but the peer pressure is so much more meaningful."

The chasm separating these parents from their children confronts many parents today. For those of us who were young before the present era of sexual freedom, the gap looks frighteningly wide. Too many of us are actually afraid of our children, feel hopeless, sure our offspring will not listen to anything we say.

How can you tell your daughter that engaging in premarital sex will give her a bad reputation when she only shrugs and wants to know with whom would her reputation be tarnished?

"Parents . . . are not so much abdicating [as] being dethroned by forces they cannot influence, much less control," says Kenneth Kenniston, MIT psychologist. Of nearly 30,000 middle-class Americans who replied to a survey conducted by *Better Homes & Gardens* magazine, 75 percent felt that the American family is in real trouble and 58 percent said that America is not as good a place to raise children as it was ten or fifteen years ago.

Readers of *Better Homes & Gardens* do not represent the entire United States, of course, but their opinions do mirror a large segment. The results of the questionnaire cannot be dismissed; they reflect the concern troubling many parents today.

We want to give our children strong support, but we feel confused by rapidly changing mores, expanding options in life-styles, and, especially, changing sexual attitudes. Nowhere is this more evident than when matters between parent and child touch on sex.

The trick here is timing. Too often we start too late in the lifelong process of imparting sexual understanding to our children, and then suddenly we find ourselves in a crisis situation—perhaps heading toward a school-age pregnancy. Where do we begin?

In the first three years of life, infants learn to love by the way they are handled. The loving touch, the back rub, the pat on the hand, a good hug—all add to words of approval. Both mothers and fathers can help their growing child develop human attachments and responses to physical and emotional closeness in warm family situations. Babies thrive as parents build a firm foundation for the child's acceptance of himself as a sexual being. We are all sexual beings from the time we are born until we die.

Babies begin life exploring their bodies, discovering each part with wonder and pleasure. As they test various possibilities, they discover a pleasurable sensation when they manipulate their genitals. This is natural. From the start, an important message is conveyed by how the parents handle this interest. A parent reacting with tension may instill in the child the idea that the sexual part of the body is bad or nasty.

Masturbation is part of nearly every child's experience. It is the result of curiosity and the search for pleasure and comfort in one's own body. These needs persist beyond infancy through the growng years. A calm and open attitude can help the child establish a guilt-free feeling toward masturbation and thus enhance acceptance of human sexuality.

It is, of course, true that we must teach our children control over their sexual behavior. But we must do this keeping in mind that our children's important sexual image of themselves depends for a major part on the messages they sense from our behavior. It will be hard to deal with masturbation casually until we totally rid ourselves of old hang-ups and myths about the subject.

By the time our children are ready for kindergarten, they should know that pregnancy, not the stork, precedes childbirth. This quite naturally leads to the information that a baby grows inside the mother. The story of the miracle of birth can unfold before the child is 8, and from there it is possible to build a foundation for knowledge of human sexual relations.

Parents who find themselves unable to deal with their 8-year-old's questions might feel better giving them a straightforward book like Peter Mayle's *Where Did I Come From?* (see Resource Guide) or other relevant books including those listed in the 1978 Sex Information and Education Council of the U.S. (SIECUS) publication "Human Sexuality: Books for Everyone." (See Resource Guide.) If you can, read such books with your child, answering questions and stimulating discussion. Your child will know if he is embarrassing you—children have a sixth sense about that—and he may stop asking although far from satisfied. If in fact he doesn't ask, look for an opportunity to give him essential information anyway.

In a Cambridge-based 1977 survey by the Project on Human Sexual Development, funded by John D. Rockefeller III, The Cleveland Foundation, The Carnegie Corporation, and others, 1,400 parents in Cleveland, Ohio, were interviewed personally. It was found that "by and large parents are not talking about sexuality at all. They're waiting for their children to ask. But what often happens is that the kids get the nonverbal message that sex is a forbidden subject."

Another significant survey involving participants aged 21 through 60 is the Sex Attitude and Knowledge Survey recently completed for the Population Institute by four experts familiar with the psychological approach to adolescent behavior. In conjunction with representatives from churches and youth organizations, three-day workshops were held in Seattle, Des Moines, and Cleveland to promote sex education. Before the first session, workshop members ranging in education from high school graduates to those with post-graduate degrees answered two questionnaires, one testing information about, and the other attitudes toward, sex. Of the respondents, 68 percent were female and 32 percent male. When the workshop study course was completed, participants were again asked the same questions, as recorded in the Resource Guide at the back of this book. You may wish to turn to these questions now, and again upon completion of the text, to test for your personal variations in knowledge, attitude, and opinion "before" and "after."

The habit of open discussion with the young cannot come too early, says Dr. Sarrel of Yale. Beginning in early childhood, opportunities present themselves. Perhaps your daughter comes to you to ask why she doesn't have a penis; you now have a perfect opportunity to talk to her easily and naturally about sex. Between the ages of 8 to 12 is a good time to make clear what happens when sperm is permitted to meet egg. At this age, emotions connected with puberty have not yet complicated a child's acceptance of sex. Appropriate teaching at school can fortify and coordinate what is being learned at home during these years.

The Connecticut State Department of Education

conducted a survey in 1968 which remains a basic resource today. Five thousand schoolchildren between kindergarten and the twelfth grade were asked what questions about sex, reproduction, and health were important
to them. The children and their teachers then recommended how best these questions could be answered.
This landmark study, *Teach Us What We Want to Know*
(see Resource Guide), can enlighten parents about how
to deal with questions their children pose at each grade
level. Using sources such as this and other excellent ones
available, parents can also help their children in their early
years learn how to give love and tenderness and to learn
to be comfortable with their sexual identity.

Sexual identity—gender identity—is not just something that is ordained at birth, but a role *played* out because of a child's social experiences in the family. Children take their values about expressing intimacy and affection from parents. Gender identity is usually established at the latest by 3 years of age. From infancy, a
child's sense of belonging to one or the other of the two
sexes is conveyed not only by words but by parental attitudes. Other influences add to children's perceptions of
what is considered appropriate gender role behavior
during later years. Today many parents no longer limit
activities to stereotyped roles or segregate boys and girls
into like-sex groups. I emphasize this since the "new sex
education" moves beyond the older concept dominated
by the biological and reproductive approach, toward a
larger view of sex roles which enhances interpersonal
growth. The attitudes or viewpoints which people hold
about being a man or a woman are a basic dynamic of
life. If, as parents, we pass on over-restrictive or conflicting attitudes about what it means to be a boy or girl, we

may hamper the ultimate sexual development of the adolescent.

Parents find it more difficult to talk to their preteen-agers, even though they agree that this responsibility belongs in the home. Yet if they wish to impart information and values, it is important to reach their boys and girls *before* they are outside the influence of their families. Are there problems with which the perceptive parent can help? While problems for both male and female are associated with their growing maturity, each requires a separate approach.

Frequent among problems needing patience and understanding by parents of boys is a growth rate that is too fast or too slow. The early bloomer may suffer from a voice that croaks out of control while his classmates still sing in a soprano. He may feel awkward, bigger than the other boys, and usually will sit in the back seat of the classroom.

Suffering from delayed puberty can be equally painful as the boy anxiously awaits the first sign of pubic hair or the growth spurt that characterizes his friends. The troubled boy's unwillingness to acknowledge his anxiety blocks parental attempts at reassurance. A father may be rebuffed if he asks a direct question. Showing awareness of the sensitive situation in some more indirect way— "You're not going out for soccer anymore"—may bring forth an admission: "I'm just too small for the team." Since late maturity has a tendency to run in families, a father's admission to having had the same experience may open up the lines of communication. The worried adolescent seeing a glimmer of hope in the fact that Dad lived through the same fears plaguing him may expose his misery more freely. The father should avoid rushing in too fast, but should rather create an atmosphere for later relaxed discussion, realizing that the real question is: "Am I different?"

This is a good opportunity to explain the facts of different rates of growth—that not everyone can be in the middle, nor is it a race to sexual maturity. Histories of boys who started behind and ended towering over their friends help the late bloomer to avoid shyness and the inadequacies he feels around girls. He can be spared acute anguish if he can be convinced he is not, as he fears, weird. The parent who is aware and at ease can help a son through this difficult time which, if not handled sensitively, could hinder the boy's emotional development.

We may also want to reassure our sons of this age that a small penis does not mean that they are less male or that they must expect to give or get less satisfaction and fulfillment in lovemaking. Likewise, when unexpected erections occur, a boy should be assured that this is normal. It is usually easy to discuss these problems in general terms as well-known, unwarranted anxieties of men so that any needling by peers will not bruise a son's sense of adequacy.

Few boys are prepared for wet dreams. These ejaculatory experiences during sleep can be frightening. Dr. Sarrel remembers interviewing a 79-year-old man who still clearly recalled his first nighttime emission because of his fear that he was bleeding to death.

He turned on the light to see what had happened and in so doing woke his grandmother in the next room. It was she who reassured him in the most natural possible way.

"It's a sign you're becoming a man," she told him,

and they both went back to bed and to sleep. He has never forgotten it.

Approximately 90 percent of all boys masturbate. This is another area in which parental attitudes are extremely important from earliest childhood. In the older boy, masturbation has an erotic connotation which makes the practice harder for the parent to accept as normal. Yet all medical experts regard it as a healthy release of tension. If masturbation were abnormal, then most of the people in the world would be abnormal.

Many parents may remember when masturbation was called self-abuse and will recall the world of outmoded ideas wrapped up in this term. Who knows what kind of misinformation is still being given out in school locker rooms about the dangers of a perfectly normal habit? College students in large numbers consult psychiatrists about masturbation, suffering needless anxiety. Many report that their fathers have taught them that masturbation is a sin.

"Fathers could save their sons immeasurable guilt and misery, and sometimes even serious mental illness, if all they did was to accomplish just one specific item of sex education: the reassurance that masturbation is normal and harmless," says Dr. Warren Gadpaille, former vice-president of the American Association of Sex Educators, Counselors and Therapists (AASECT).

Worry about masturbation is probably only equalled in the world of young boys by worry over homosexuality. Here is another area in which parents can help. Fear of homosexuality is deeply imbedded in adult men as well as in boys, and parents must make every effort not to put undue pressure on their sons to be "really masculine" because of their own often unconscious anxieties.

The message from such parents often comes through as, "I am not sure about you, and I want you to show me by your behavior that you are really a boy." If a young boy knows that his parents are questioning his sexuality, he will question it himself. Boys who suffer unspoken doubts about their proclivities could withdraw from relationships with girls or enter into a career of irresponsible behavior to prove their masculinity.

Parents who realize that same-sex friendshps are healthy will relax in the knowledge that this is a natural part of growing up. Parents also should look with equally benign interest in their sons' choice of activities once regarded as feminine such as cooking, sewing, and dancing.

We must warn our sons to ignore certain common myths by reassuring them that a pass from a homosexual does not mean they have "the homosexual look," and that one or two same-sex experiences does not define them as homosexuals.

One school counselor told me of a midnight phone call from a high-school senior who was desperate to confess that he had just had a second homosexual experience, which convinced him he was doomed. His distress was so acute that he made references to suicide. As the counselor tried to calm the boy's fears, explaining that sexual preferences are not defined until adulthood, the boy heard his father's car in the driveway and abruptly hung up the phone with the words, "Do you suppose he will suspect?" If only he could have turned to an understanding father at that critical time!

The Project on Human Sexual Development emphasizes that there is also room for improvement in the sexual information girls receive. Although most mothers were not satisfied with the way their mothers had explained menstruation to them, they have done little to educate themselves in order to ease their daughters' introduction to this significant sign of the onset of puberty. Timing is important here, for today's daughter will probably begin at an earlier age than her mother did: 12 to 13 is average age, which means that some girls start as early as 10. A booklet with explicit diagrams of the reproductive system as it relates to the menstrual cycle helps. One good example, *How to Talk to Your Teenagers About Something That's Not Easy to Talk About* (see Resource Guide), is informative and honest. A healthy attitude toward menstruation, with an emphasis on keeping up one's usual activities during that time, should be encouraged by a mother even though she may have been restricted in her own freedom in keeping with earlier customs. Medical advice now allows swimming, running, tennis, and other sports. The old taboos are disappearing. If discomfort or disorder is serious enough to consult a physician, this would also be a good time to acquaint your daughter with the pelvic examination associated with good reproductive health, now and in the future.

The problem of growth that is too fast or too slow at puberty is also a major one for girls. The "adolescent slouch" is often an attempt by the early bloomer to appear more nearly the size of classmates or to conceal well-developed breasts that make last year's sweaters bulge. Other girls suffer anxiety awaiting the growth of breasts which many girls in the gym locker room are already beginning to show. As they worry "Am I normal?" and await signs of the first menstrual period, many importune their mothers prematurely to buy bras and equipment in preparation for the expected period. Sensitive to her daughter's need for reassurance that she will soon join the ranks of envied friends who have "it," the wise mother will respond by accompanying her daughter to purchase a starter bra which the stores offer for girls of this age. Such a bra may be used and stuffed with cotton balls—do not ridicule if your daughter delights in her profile, now satisfying to her, as she wears her first long dress. When the day comes on which she first menstruates, you will be glad you have so thoroughly prepared her for the significance of "being a woman," a status she has so eagerly anticipated.

Your involvement in preparing her for her first menstruation will open the door for an honest discussion of sexual intercourse. Too many parents remain silent on the subjects of intercourse or premarital sex. The role of the parent must include acceptance of discussing the erotic aspects of human relationships. Providing guidance to their children on how to deal with their awakening sexual feelings is vital for parents, and should be possible to convey within their own belief system. Ideally, of course the task of encouraging teens to think about and develop standards for their own behavior should start before the teen years bring pressure they are unready to face with their own value system.

Through open communication a mother can protect her daughter against baffling misinformation. It is quite natural, once she has reached adolescence, to give a young girl a general definition of contraception—that its purpose, whatever the method, is to prevent the sperm cell from uniting with the egg. Reliable methods available through prescription only (IUD, diaphragm, pills) as well as an effective non-prescription combination (condom plus foam) available over the counter may be described in general categories to stimulate later questioning as she becomes more sophisticated, or to combat any false information she may receive.

Ignorance is one of the major causes of pregnancy among the very young. Not all aspects of sex can be covered in a single session, with a sigh of relief at a hard job accomplished. If the family atmosphere treats sex as a normal, integral part of life, natural questions, calmly answered, will avoid distortion. Sex will be perceived from the start as a healthy process, and this will continue as adolescents grow and gain life experience.

Studies show that the proportion of girls who masturbate is smaller than boys. At this stage, parental fear that it gives forbidden sexual pleasure, according to the Sexual Development Study, adds a new dimension that disturbs at least half of the Cleveland parent group who participated in this investigation. A hint of parental intolerance can arouse all the feelings of guilt that so long clustered around this normal activity. It can awaken self-doubts at the very stage when a daughter needs most assurance of her normality. And of course masturbation is certainly less dangerous than the potential consequences of genital play with boys in the very early teens, when the rise in unintended pregnancy is greatest today.

Similarly, parental fears of lesbian development during adolescence can be exaggerated and cause unnecessary stress at a sensitive time in a girl's life cycle when she has not yet established her eventual sexual identity.

Each family develops its own way of dealing with the sexuality of its children. There is no single moral code that is accepted by a majority of people in America today. Discussion between parents and a young son, aware for the first time of the new and strange reactions of his body, may be out of the question in some families, or at best be on extremely touchy ground. Talk of sex on a personal basis may be too delicate a matter to undertake unless the underlying fabric of the family relationship is strong. One of the most pertinent findings of the Project on Human Sexual Development was that many parents feel it is unwise to impress their values on their children. Elizabeth M. Roberts, Executive Director of the Project, described the dilemma this way: "Parents are having trouble reconciling what they feel they should do in the way of sex education with what they feel they can do. Many parents find themselves confused about the accuracy of their own values and life-style for their children." Other parents who have discussed values with their growing children experience disappointment when they feel they have failed to communicate. Parents can do no more than open the door to free discussion; reaching agreement is not necessary if we try to build trust by an honest expression of our own opinions. As difficult as this is, in the face of 1 million teenage pregnancies each year there are many who think it is the duty of parents to try.

A little dialogue between parents and their teenage daughters and sons about condoms alone could have a real impact on the millions of teenage males taking a chance of unplanned parenthood every year. Parents might suggest to their adolescents that the sense of security good contraception offers is a positive step toward creating a good relationship. A couple's working together to avoid pregnancy adds trust to the sex act. Parents can stress that sex for the purpose of procreation occurs only a few times in a lifetime. The rest of the time, they can point out, it is a means of expressing love, closeness, and mutual pleasure, and of escaping, temporarily, the individual's essential loneliness. Parents can emphasize that it is a help not to have to think, at these moments, of the possible consequences of an unprotected act. Many parents may wish to stress their belief that a sexual relationship is more meaningful within the marriage commitment or that it should be enjoyed only within the marriage commitment.

Dr. Mary Calderone, president of SEICUS, sums up the parental role as follows: "You must take stock of where they came from sexually. Ambiguous, unsure; . . . repressive, conflicting or rapidly shifting attitudes about gender role behavior in the parents . . . can be imprinted on the child's life pattern [as] insecurity, doubt, compulsiveness, feelings of incompetence or, especially today and especially in the United States, overweighting of one or another aspect of sexuality."

Don't confuse puberty with adolescence. They are part of the same thing—growing up—but different parts of it. Adolescence is the psychological and social process initiated by puberty, a hormonal growth process. The biological changes involved in puberty are stressful, making adolescence a struggle for mastery over changed biological states. An understanding of this may cast light on the family strains characteristic of that period.

I know a man who lectures often before audiences of parents and has developed a brief biographical sketch to let his listeners know a little something about him. He always ends it with the wry addendum, "My wife and I are the parents of two teenage children who live alone at our house." The words never fail to evoke uneasy, sympathetic laughter.

Even if you as parents have painstakingly built a bridge between yourselves and your children founded on easy mutual respect, a day may well arrive when your friendly, open, compliant child changes into a rebellious, secretive teenager. Countless parents have looked on in stunned disbelief at the dramatic changes which affect the personality of a son or a daughter, seemingly almost overnight. The alchemy of puberty, as Dr. Joan Morgenthau, director of Adolescent Health Services and professor of pediatrics at Mount Sinai School of Medicine, calls it, has wounded many a mother and father. It is, says Morgenthau, as if some secret hormonal spigot had suddenly been turned on.

This is a bad time, as any junior-high-school principal knows. Some, in their sympathy for the parents of their students, have arranged with psychiatrists to address PTA meetings to elucidate this quite normal Dr. Jekyll-Mr. Hyde transformation. Speaking at such a meeting of parents at a boys' school in Washington, D.C., one psychiatrist remarked: "Think of your son's physical system as a smoothly running electrical circuit. In childhood, all the lines function sweetly, plugging into home and Mommy. Now comes puberty and the strengthening of the sex drive. What is more unsuitable for home and mother than overriding sex drives? The entire circuit blows and what you get is loud music, slammed doors, a rupture of a smoothly running relationship."

One way of coping with the rages and moodiness of adolescents, caught between childhood and adulthood as they are, is to treat your teenager as an adult as he or she "earns" that treatment. At the same time, a parent should help the child forge the tools necessary to achieve the tasks of adolescence—independence and responsible decision making—in a confusing world.

Perhaps the most important tool an adolescent needs is self-esteem. This can help him say no, if he chooses, when everybody else is saying yes. Peer pressure can make an adolescent feel like the only one who didn't get tapped for the club. Teenagers must learn to ask themselves, "Is this right for me?" They must do things because they really want to do them, not because their friends are doing them or a potential sex partner wants them to.

How can parents help sons and daughters build the self-esteem and other inner supports that Dr. Catherine Chilman, Professor of the University of Wisconsin, School of Social Welfare, reports research studies find lacking in many involved in premarital sex? Not all ways of reaching the sexually active teenager are direct and overt. In the world of the adolescent, having low educational goals and poor school marks rank high on the list of reasons to turn elsewhere for satisfactions. Many who flounder in the school systems have abandoned hope and the incentive to plan. By encouraging young people to participate in extracurricular activities, gain job experience, and generally broaden their interests, parents can bolster an adolescent's flagging sense of self.

Parents concerned that their children's friends may promote such commonly held risk-taking attitudes as "I'll be lucky and not get pregnant," might tactfully seek to expose sons and daughters to new associations through youth serving organizations, club activities, tennis, or swimming lessons. They might also plan outings to jazz concerts, movies, museums, or a sporting event, both as a way of being together and of reminding teenagers that there is a world apart from their peers.

What about the 50 percent of boys and girls who do not elect during their teen years to enter a sexual relationship? They may be looking for parental help in resisting pressures from one or a group of peers. Such simple reinforcements as "give us a call and we'll pick you up" or "tell them your parents won't let you" can supply adolescents with ways to say "no." Catherine Chilman suggests that parents might give further verbal support to young people who have decided early intercourse is unwise by suggesting: "I think it's better to wait until you're older because sex is best when it's part of a committed, grownup relationship."

But remember—not only must an adolescent feel free to differ from his peers, he should also feel the decision is his, not that of a manipulative parent. Domineering parents with little understanding cause more sexual rebellion ending in pregnancy than most people imagine.

Karen is an example of a teenager caught in one such trap. Daughter of a prominent family, she grew up in a home that drew its standards from stern discipline. Her father in particular kept strict account of her comings and goings. When he turned over to her a tool shed next to the garage for her birthday, he felt at liberty to peek in the door whenever he passed the snug retreat Karen had made for herself. He was, in short, spying on her life.

In the shed, Karen, just 15, was playing house, reading her books, entertaining her friends. Dad, constantly checking on her, found nothing to upset him, but the feeling of being watched gradually made Karen edgy. At first she was irritated; then she grew angry. In the end, she created the scenario her father had feared he might uncover. She began to use the shed for sex encounters.

By now alarmed, her parents sent her to camp and later to a series of boarding schools. But she ran away from all of those and eventually became a sex adventurer. In an interview with a sex counselor, much later, she complained that she had been treated like a child or, as the counselor put it later, as a possession, not a person. "I'd do anything to get back at my father," she said bitterly.

Another part of the process of raising children is directed toward allowing them to exercise their independence.

Since a parent cannot always stand beside them, making decisions for them, the best thing is to equip them to make decisions for themselves. Trust them.

The process of raising children whose decisions you *can* trust begins early, when very young children are encouraged to make little decisions: what clothes to wear, what to eat in a restaurant. Older children can make more important decisions such as how much TV to watch, how to schedule time, or how to spend their allowance—all with the family expressing pride and approval. The ability to make decisions will become a habit and a skill which will lead to well-informed, constructive decisions about human relationships.

The new Values Clarification Training, which includes a range of ethical alternatives of which sexual behavior is one consideration, has been adopted by progressive schools in some cities and provides classroom experiences in which children can learn to make responsible choices. The problems in the training are tuned to each age level, but a typical one in high school, selected from a popular guide to values clarification, *Helping Your Child Learn Right From Wrong* (see Resource Guide), is that of a 15-year-old boy who finds himself sexually aroused merely by sitting next to a girl while watching television. From the open discussion that follows, the students may explore responsibility for actions. The solutions offered by others make it clear there are always alternatives.

Decision-making exercises are also now available in Parent Effectiveness Training courses offered by some PTAs and also for volunteers training in sex education fields. Through such learning experiences parents are introduced to ways in which they can help their children by examining options together, participating in games of problem solving. As parent and child come up with different choices in hypothetical cases, each can develop mutual respect for the alternative the other has chosen. This method can help parents help their children develop their value system without preaching or lecturing, shaming or blaming. Many children who have enjoyed this approach at home or at school are proving that child-parent alienation is not inevitable. *Values in Sexuality* by Eleanor S. Morrison and Mila Underhill Price (see Resource Guide) is helpful in transmitting this new approach to sex education.

To bring up a child in today's world is obviously not easy. As always, the gap between generations seems to make of us, parents and children, two different species. We scarcely seem to speak the same language. These mutual efforts at testing values may help us get to know each other's worlds.

A distinguished authority on adolescent sexuality, while preparing a paper on sex talks between mothers and daughters, asked her own daughter where to insert pertinent information. "It doesn't matter," the girl said. "My friends won't read it anyway."

If even the experts have difficulties in making themselves heard, is it surprising that many parents experience a failure of rapport somewhere along the way?

Should you find yourself unable to get through to your teenager, as happens to the best of us, try to keep in mind that this is natural. Adolescence is marked by an intense need to separate from one's parents, a need which may take dramatic forms. The wise parent will recognize such histrionics as a sign of a normal growth process, a phase aimed at achieving the personal independence necessary for healthy adulthood.

Remember, in this trying period, that patience pays off. Continue to show your adolescents that you love and support them, that there is a place for them in the family whenever they will accept it—that you care enough both to help them achieve their independence and guide them in their search. The teenager may be greatly in need of the help that clear, firm, mild discipline can provide. In an effort to be broadminded and non-interfering, parents should not be reluctant to provide controls at a time when adolescents need a significant measure of support.

4

Breaking the Silence Barrier

"Parents must communicate to young people that sex relationships are basically human relationships," says Mary Lee Tatum, teacher of ground-breaking human sexuality courses in Falls Church, Virginia. "Sexual behavior depends upon a sense of self and a process of decision making. Children can be given an opportunity to learn, within the family, good decision-making skills. Good decisions can be enhanced by good communication of values within the family."

Baffled, uneasy, unsure of ourselves, we haven't been doing much to bridge the yawning difference between our children's world and our own. Yet there are smoke signals from the other side of the gap, small signs that some of our children would not be averse to accepting our advice.

Dr. Philip Sarrel, medical director of the Yale University Student Health Center, administered a questionnaire to Yale's incoming freshmen to evaluate what they knew about sex and how they had found it out. Only 30 percent said they had had any guidance in these matters from their families and the anonymous questionnaires seemed to suggest that such guidance would not have gone amiss.

Dr. Sarrel isn't the only one who feels that young people today would welcome frank and open discussion of sex in their homes. Dr. Marion Howard, director of the Emory Grady Hospital Teen Services Program in Atlanta, Georgia, which adopts a comprehensive approach to adolescents aged 16 or younger, says she has observed that most of the 1,000 sexually active adolescents in their early teens receiving services from the program wish they could talk to their parents about it. "They are wishful," says Dr. Howard. "One young girl getting birth control assistance was especially regretful she could not tell her mother what she was doing. 'I'm going to tell her later,' she said to me. 'Someday. And she'll be proud of me.' "

There are others who see indications that home discussion of sexual matters would be acceptable to the young. Possibly parental advice is not as unwelcome as many parents believe. Dr. Gisela Konopka, director of the Center for Youth Development and Research at the University of Minnesota, says that when her organization asked more than 200 young people in several schools what they wanted most, "The youngsters seem to be yearning for communication with their parents. And somehow," says Konopka, "they did not feel they were really getting it."

Have we been failing them all along? There is no possible way to know how things would have turned out if more parents had had closer relationships with their adolescents instead of being self-absorbed in their own identity crises.

"The inaccessible father" has become a key phrase in reporting studies of parent-child relations. The tradition of mother as the caretaker persists in most American homes, since the father's role continues to have little part in the daily routine of child care and may consist largely of admonitions. Many children perceive their fathers as distant and disinterested. It is no small wonder that paternal failure to discuss sexuality, particularly the erotic aspects, appears as a common factor in investigations of how and where children receive sex information or form attitudes toward their own sexuality. As parental roles become more flexible in practice as they have in theory, fathers may gain satisfaction from assuming responsibility for their children's development in this and other areas from earliest childhood.

HEW has issued a pamphlet, *Teenage Pregnancy, Everybody's Problem* (see Resource Guide), in which it quotes a mother who, on learning her daughter is pregnant, cries in agony: "She said she was afraid I would find the pills. Afraid? I would have helped her . . . arranged for her to see our family doctor . . . rather than see her like this."

Ah, but would she? More likely she would have been unbelieving, angry, panic-stricken, and recriminatory in turn. Almost nothing more difficult is asked of parents today than to adjust to the sexuality of their daughters. Brought up as we were in a world which at least pretended to value virginity, few mothers and even fewer fathers can face the fact that their daughter is engaged in sexual activity outside marriage. The jump from acceptance of this fact to seeming to actually abet it with birth control information provokes as wide differences of opinion as politics does. How many mothers, for instance, would act as Irene Chisholm (not her real name) did when her 16-year-old daughter came to her for help when she had missed a period?

In such a situation anguish can never be completely wiped away, but Irene understood that this was not the moment for bemoaning what might have been. Instead, she asked her daughter if she would like to see her gynecologist, and when her daughter agreed, she made an appointment. Two days before the appointment, her daughter reported that it had all been a false alarm.

Many mothers would have left it there, but Irene asked her daughter to consider whether she would like to keep the appointment anyway. Aware that sex, once tried, is difficult to give up, she asked her daughter if she thought it was possible it would all happen again. Her daughter replied that she feared it might, and asked her mother to go with her to see the gynecologist. They went together to keep an appointment in which the daughter learned for the first time how to avoid pregnancy.

Irene's nonjudgmental attitude—difficult as it was for her to achieve, since somehow she was admitting that sex outside procreation was "all right"—cemented understanding between mother and daughter.

Many, many parents cannot overcome a feeling of repugnance at the idea of being the ones to make birth control services available to their daughters, in what might be regarded tacit approval of illicit sex. Parents might remember, however, the Planned Parenthood study cited earlier indicating that most adolescents seek clinical services well *after* their sexual activity has begun. The hazards of the unprotected interim could give parents concern.

But a representative share of parents today have broken away from those who continue to believe that a permissive era compounds its errors by offering ways to avoid pregnancy.

Dr. Phillips Cutright, sociology professor at Indiana University, in his article "The Teenage Sexual Revolution and the Myth of an Abstinent Past" (see Resource Guide), supports them with the following succinct statement: "Access to effective medically supervised contraception . . . is no more likely to encourage teenage promiscuity than denial of access has been to discourage adolescent sexual activity." If a teenager does not practice abstinence, the effective use of contraception becomes essential despite intrinsic barriers. We are asking teenagers to use a cold, objective method—often disruptive—in the highly charged subjective, emotional situation of the sex act. Many feel that we are sailing against the wind by asking them to do something against their nature—that is, to think ahead and accept their own sexuality. Many insist this destroys romantic spontaneity and interferes with pleasure in a loving relationship.

To talk with our adolescents, to maintain a relationship which makes it possible for what we say to matter to them, it is necessary for us to remember what kind of a world many of us live in. We were brought up in a society which lived by different standards, and it will be easier going if we make it clear to them that we understand that things have changed.

In the Youth Values Project, funded by The Population Institute and the New York Charities Aid Association, teenagers serving as "consultants" to the Director,

Susan Ross, devised a questionnaire which points up that the new mores give marriage a different priority in our children's world than in ours. Only 26 percent of the girls surveyed in the Project and 24 percent of the males rated marriage a very important goal in their lives. This does not, however, mean a choice in favor of indiscriminate sex behavior. It is far more likely to mean sexual loyalty to one partner, though the unions may follow each other in rapid succession, like Hollywood marriages. Such relationships have become so common that at the last census, a total of 1,500,000 liaisons of this type were reported, a 100 percent increase in the last ten years.

The moralists to the contrary, sex without marriage is gaining social acceptance. The Gallup Poll reveals that over the last ten years 16 percent more of us have come to accept the idea as a way of life, bringing the total to 48 percent. We are talking here about almost half the country, a representative sample of America.

This example of liberal action represents one more reason why the adolescents involved in nonmarital sexual relationships do not feel they are doing anything morally wrong. In a national poll querying a representative sample of 1,044 people taken by the Yankelovich organization, 60 percent of young respondents feel that sex without marriage is perfectly acceptable. The general population disagreed, with 63 percent saying it is morally wrong for teenagers to have sexual relations. Even more revealing, of those participating aged 35-49—the age group most likely to be parents of teenagers—72 percent disapproved of premarital teenage sex, an indication of the gap in values parents and their children must cross.

Even harder for a generation of parents to swallow is the shocking fact that sociologists say some adolescents engaging in sexual liaisons actually want to conceive.

"It's as if it were just the thing to do," says Dr. Francis Hutcher of the Temple Hospital Family Planning Center in Philadelphia. "In earlier decades, pregnancy, even in wedlock, was considered something to conceal as far as humanly possible. Young girls who found themselves pregnant outside of marriage regarded it as a disaster and took a hopeless, fatalistic view of the future. Today, pregnancy, in some circles, is instant prestige and, if there's trouble at home, it is the very best way to spite parents."

"People treat you like you are somebody when you're pregnant," said one young girl, surveying her bulging stomach with satisfaction.

"How can I persuade her she's ruining her life when her classmates seem almost envious?" says her mother.

We cannot bridge the gap between our adolescents and ourselves unless we also understand that many offer sexual favors to attain popularity. Most vulnerable of all to peer pressure, to accepting aggressive sex advances from boys with no semblance of love are the girls under 15. Countrywide, half of all Planned Parenthood services are provided now to girls under 19. Sexual discussions with these adolescents must be based on understanding some of the forces driving them into these tragic early pregnancies.

Only with some basic knowledge of the fragile structure of their mores can we effectively approach our children for an open sexual discussion. Even then it will not be easy. There are no guidelines, no set rules for sexual behavior in our society in flux. Most parents will probably have to tailor their approach in such conversations to what they know of themselves and their own children. The Project on Human Sexual Development discovered that when it comes to speaking about the erotic manifestations of sex, parents become "defensive and confused. The delicate balance between the unsure beliefs of parents and what they want their children to believe seems hard to achieve." Of the Cleveland parents involved in the Project, 80 percent would welcome the idea of community-based discussion groups for themselves which would help them clarify their own value beliefs about such subjects as premarital sex, contraception, and masturbation.

Other cities have found it useful for parents to join a group of other parents wrestling with the same difficulties, if only to make it clear that no parent of an adolescent is really alone. In such discussions parents can both measure other methods against their own and join forces to enforce rules so that no child can say to her parent, "But Sandy down the block is allowed to invite boys home even when her parents are out."

In Washington, D.C., parents of children in the city's 34 independent schools founded the Parents Council of Washington for the guidance of parents. Working with faculty committees from each school, they hammered out with the professionals and consulting experts guidelines about curfew hours, what drinks should be served in any cooperating home, who should drive the car on a date—myriad small details which often have a bearing on sexual encounters. A booklet, *Changing Trends*, produced through their cooperative efforts, is distributed to parents who wish to discuss these issues with their children.

If you organize such a group, you can discuss ways to suggest limits from the first, with the purpose of finding ways to avoid situations which would lead to testing these limits. If several parents band together and agree their daughters might say to their dates, "My parents don't allow me to go on late car drives" or solitary picnics, campouts, or have anyone join them when they are baby-sitting; this way no one will feel different and much trouble will have been anticipated and possibly averted. Not surprisingly, with the increase of parental activity outside the home, the most common location of accidental conception is the empty bedroom of an absent adult. The proof of this comes from scientific investigation of the "geography" of teenage conception. Laying down house rules about visitors in the absence of adults is something parents might therefore consider.

Many organizations stand ready to cooperate with or absorb groups of parents worried about sexual mores and the gap which lies between them and their adolescent children. The Ys have offered parents peer discussion groups for some time, and so have 4-H clubs, churches, women's clubs, and the Red Cross. Parents feel keenly that they have a need to catch up with the world, and the service organizations are aware of this. The past five years have brought matters into the open which would seldom have been discussed earlier even in the privacy of the home. Your church or synagogue could also be active in this field, helping to keep communication flowing.

Remember, rejection and omission teach, too, saying plainly that parents feel sexual matters are not fit subjects of discussion. This is a bad message for any child to absorb. On the other hand, professional teachers must not shirk their role. They have a valuable part to play. "School kids," says Dr. Margaret Jones of the Coalition for Children and Youth, "are not the same ones we dealt with as parents in our own culture." The interaction of adolescents is a daily scene for teachers and they often know what the young are thinking.

Parental self-doubt is so widespread that the Institute for Family Research and Education undertook a 3-year project to help parents and their communities learn how to organize courses in sex education. Drs. Sol Gordon and Kathleen Everly, along with other experts, directed the project from Syracuse. It aimed to help parents become more effective educators of their own children. Over 1,000 parents participated in programs offered by 70 community leaders trained through the project. Out of this project grew a training manual for organizers entitled "Community Family Life Education Programs for Parents" that is available to communities who wish guidance in organizing programs based on the conclusions from the research study (see Resource Guide). It covers such questions as selecting content of training sessions, how to select key community leaders for initial training, how to enlist the support of essential groups, and how to encourage continued community interest and involvement in sex education.

The manual also contains recommendations for parents on how to deal with their own feelings about sexuality, provides opportunities for such discussion, and helps defuse common myths. It could be invaluable to any citizen or professional group seeking to improve communication on this subject geared to their own local situation.

The study revealed that three basic myths undermine parents' self-confidence in their attempts to discuss sex with their children. The first of these, and perhaps the most erroneous, is the idea that parents must know everything there is to know about sex. Parents generally seem to have a compulsive need to be perfect in their children's eyes and to lay down rules for behavior rather than open a general discussion, because of this need to appear infallible. Eighty percent of a sample group of parents confess to this error.

Realistically, nobody can know it all, especially in this fast-changing world. If we admit this, we are not really putting ourselves down; we are building understanding.

The study also finds that we feel the children will not listen unless we ourselves are very avant-garde. Nothing could be more wrong. We should honor our own values or how can we expect our children to? We should honor them, but not necessarily impose them on our offspring, for theirs is a world different from ours, one in transition, through which they will have to find their way as individuals.

The study also confirmed the fact that most parents don't feel comfortable discussing sex with their children. Probably our own parents didn't teach us about sex and we find ourselves uneasy breaking new ground. The news is that it is okay to feel uncomfortable. This will be another bridge between us and our uncomfortable children.

The study strongly suggests that in any sex education program for parents, the group should probably start by clearing up a few misconceptions that have prevented, in the past, a desire to discuss sex with one's children from being translated into a useful dialogue.

You may still feel unready to undertake such a discussion with your child, and worry, as many bewildered parents do, "Is it because I have failed as a parent that my 15-year-old girl is having sex?" If so, it is very possible that you can point the way to experts whose help might be accepted more effectively than your own at this time. If you have not made a habit of discussing anything with your adolescent except what to have for breakfast and whether the car needs gas, you may well have a hard time starting in discussing sex.

You might also call upon the skills of school counselors if you plan to share the job with someone else. Some school personnel are increasingly meeting situations involving sexual problems and are in a position to study them firsthand. They may be well trained and their familiarity with adolescent vernacular and mores may make them highly acceptable as advisers.

Many sex educators have been certified by AASECT, an organization that offers sophisticated training. It also provides consultation, tailored to the individual community interests in developing a school sex education program. Their services may be explored through the Washington, D.C., headquarters.

In seeking immediate help in sex-related problems, you might also consider your family doctor or a specially trained nurse or social worker if their area of interest extends to the whole person. Since this quality may be lacking in such busy people, it may be well to arrange a discussion beforehand to be sure that your philosophies on these delicate matters are in tune.

Occasionally it is a teacher, cleric, or a club leader with no special degree in psychology, a person who simply possesses the gift of empathy, who turns out to be the one whom your child will respect, trust, and speak openly with about sexual problems. When the Youth Values Project was completed, the young people who worked on the project were asked whose names they wanted in the acknowledgments. Some august names were listed but, with one accord, the young people insisted that the name of a health teacher in Queens, gifted with an ability to listen and to understand the problems of the young, be added. The name of Mrs. Elaine Jacobs led all the rest. Whether or not we talk to our children ourselves or point the way to another attentive ear, we are bound to alleviate the pathetic separateness in which so many families with adolescents live. The key is communication, and however we attempt it, we must do our best to bring the subject of sex out of the shadows.

As adults we are not alone in encountering barriers to talking about sex. Lack of communication between young sexual partners can block the use of contraceptive information.

Consider, for instance, the case of Lucy, who desperately sought information about birth control from a fellow student. Her friend suggested that the first thing to do was talk with her boyfriend about which method best suited their needs. Horror-stricken, Lucy replied: "Oh no! Some things are just too sacred to *talk* about!"

Witness, too, the young boy whose parents were aware of a particularly intense love affair in which he was obviously deeply involved. They persuaded him to go to a sex counselor for contraceptive advice. "Have you discussed this with your sex partner?" the counselor inquired. "No," replied the boy. "I really don't know her that well."

5

Behind the
Male Myth

Beyond its strictly biological aspects, the young male's role in teenage pregnancy has, for the most part, been ignored. The problems of teenage girls have dominated the minds of the medical and social scientists as well as the newscasters even though, except for the biological fact of pregnancy, boys are as vulnerable to the current shifting values and mores as the girls themselves.

Adolescent boys suffer as much confusion and anxiety over sexual matters as their partners do, says Dr. Gary Goldsmith, clinical director of health services at The Door, a comprehensive organization serving teenagers in New York City. It is even possible that they are just as vulnerable as the girls. Some have been known to weep in sex counselors' offices over the breakup of a romance they thought would last forever.

Boys seldom turn to their peers for comfort. They report their victories but not their defeats. The credo that men do not cry is still strong in our culture. Ninety percent of the fathers in the recent Cleveland study said they wanted to communicate to their sons that it was all right to cry, but admitted that they themselves never did. Boys tend to suffer in silence and try to keep their cool. The son of a friend of mine once came home from a fight with his girl and went straight to the bathroom and into the shower to muffle the sounds of his sobs.

They are vulnerable, but even from age 12 to 15 boys may have a sexual urge many times greater than girls their age. This may account for the apparent disharmony of goals between some boys and and their girl friends, says Dr. Eleanor Hamilton, sex educator. Seventy percent of boys have had intercourse by the age of 17, and by the years between 18 and 20, the male sex drive has peaked. Though this early peaking has been questioned, it is clear that teenage boys have strong sexual feelings and curiosity about sexual matters.

Nevertheless, few would argue that teenage boys are as psychologically and emotionally mature as they are sexually developed. One has only to look at the answers given by the boys themselves in a variety of studies about how their strong drives are used to doubt that they are mature enough to handle them without more adequate help from teachers, clergy, counselors, doctors, and parents.

There is no male stereotype and the profile of an adolescent male would not be easy to define. Dr. Peter Scales, a former research director of the Institute for Family Research and Sex Education, has reviewed the literature of male attitudes toward sex and contraceptive behavior and finds it surrounded with confusion, ignorance, and mythology. My own search of recent studies even discovered contradictory attitudes reflected within a single test taken by a single boy.

Anyone who looked at the interesting sex questionnaire conducted by *Seventeen* magazine in 1978 saw how changing trends have produced a crazy quilt of attitudes and expectations.

"I don't want this to get back to my girl friend," said one young man who answered the questions, "but yes, I would like to live with her." He did not, however, plan to marry her. He wanted the girl he married to be a virgin, and nearly 60 percent of the boys surveyed agreed. Yet when it came to the question "Do you expect to live with a girl before marriage?" the answers were split right down the middle.

Vague and conflicting messages emerge from shattered old beliefs and it is no wonder boys are not sure where they stand on their sexual identity, role, function, and responsibility.

The situation is further complicated by the uncertain attitude of girls. A similar national survey by *Seventeen* in 1979 asked what girls 16 to 24 "really look for in boys."

What emerges from the answers appears to put new burdens on a boy's management of his sexuality. Does he need sexual experience? Less than 10 percent of the girls would decidedly prefer to date a man who is a virgin; 25 percent would strongly prefer not to. But almost one third of the girls were "not sure how they felt on this issue." If the girls are unsure about the kinds of dates they prefer, the boys are obviously working under a handicap in trying to determine their roles.

To the question "Do you prefer a guy to take the lead in making out?" a third again were not sure, while almost 65 percent agreed that they wanted the boy to move first.

When it came to marriage, less than 20 percent would strongly prefer that their husband not be a virgin. 80 percent were not sure. Sixty-six percent are now prepared for a two-career marriage.

One area in which the girls were *not* ambivalent was in the personality traits they consider important in the man they marry. Ninety percent wanted a boy to be loving, responsible, thoughtful, considerate, and gentle—quite an order, but a definite departure from the super-masculine image that boys so often believe is required.

How are we helping our ambivalent adolescents to sort out their values?

Hardly at all. Among 1,000 sexually active teenagers surveyed by The Youth Values Project, only 22 percent said they had gleaned their knowledge of the basic biological facts from their parents. Males especially suffer—half as many males as females reported getting birth control information at home, according to a 1975 study by Dr. R. C. Sorenson.

The youth survey also revealed a definite double standard in parents' attitude toward their children's sexual encounters. Asked if their mothers would be upset if they found out they were having sex, only 28 percent of the boys replied yes, while 41 percent of the girls thought their mothers would be seriously disturbed. Fifty percent of the boys guessed their mothers "wouldn't say anything," would look on their activities as normal, or shrug and suggest birth control; only 37 percent of the girls thought their mothers would take their encounters so lightly. Paternal displeasure was even less feared. As many as 65 percent of the boys thought their fathers might either react neutrally or be secretly pleased.

Clearly, the double standard dies hard. The women's movement to the contrary, the macho image lingers. Today even infants appear in T-shirts bearing the message "macho-baby."

Since boys comprise half of every teenage pregnancy problem, it is essential to educate them. Abysmal ignorance of sex exists in the minds of many young boys. Chicago Planned Parenthood conducted a survey in 1977 of 1,000 males aged 15 to 19 and discovered that most had grown to nearly manhood still blindfolded by mind-boggling misinformation. Over 50 percent of those answering Planned Parenthood's quiz thought birth control was for girls only. Twenty-five percent checked the box suggesting it is not right to use birth control. Thirty-four percent said they thought if the girl became pregnant, it was her fault because she should have protected herself. Seventy percent thought it was right to tell a girl you love her to get her to have sex with you.

The idea of a pregnancy hadn't even crossed the mind of 40 percent of the boys during their most recent sex act—a real cause for alarm in view of the fact that consistent sexual activity without birth control includes an 80 percent chance of pregnancy. With these young males, sexual intercourse was a type of roulette. "She'll never get pregnant the first time," said one boy.

Half of over 400 sexually experienced male students in three northeastern high schools were discovered to have begun activities by the age of 13, according to a 1975 study by Dr. David and Dr. Madelon Lubin

Finkel. Their research confirmed that 25 percent used no contraceptives and an equal number relied on the ancient withdrawal method in spite of generally available condoms. Less than 11 percent reported having learned about human reproduction from a family member.

In 1978, Ann Landers reprinted a sex test for teenagers devised by five adolescents. No student working on the test was over 17, but the questions covered group sex, homosexuality, oral, and anal sex. Yet such basic knowledge as the likely time for pregnancy in a girl's menstrual cycle seemed sadly lacking. Teenagers have a desperate need to appear knowledgeable. Cool, in their vernacular, often covers mere pseudosophistication about sex.

The boys coming into Planned Parenthood of Southern Arizona know very little about reproduction or commitment in relationships, says J. Stephen Kirkpatrick, director. Study the following questions—reproduced exactly as they were written by the students themselves, high-school sophomores in Tucson public schools—and you will see the depths of sexual ignorance:

1. Is sex supposed to be kept quite? I mean should you be embarassed to talk about it to the opposite sex?

2. If it is your 3rd or 4th time for having sex then you do it again and he pulls out before he comes, do you have a good chance of getting pregnant?

3. Does coming into the clinic just to talk cost anything?

4. I've always heard that if a girl misses one pill she'll get pregnate even if she hasn't screwed.

5. Does douching have any effect after a long period of time? How old should a girl be when she starts to douche?

6. Is it true that you should go to the bathroom soon after sex to prevent infection?

7. Is it safe to have oral sex, and swallow the sperm?

8. What are those coils called? Condums?

"[Their] false bravado," says Kirkpatrick, "covers a massive lack of knowledge . . . They do not know the most basic facts . . . They are a high-risk group as far as the unplanned adolescent pregnancy goes. Their ignorance combined with their curiosity about sex makes it highly likely that they will seize the first and every opportunity to have sex with little knowledge of the probability or extent of the consequences."

One suburban high school is offering a 10-week course in Human Sexuality, a seminar through which it hopes to get to discover why high-school students engage in sex. The boys in this seminar complained that girls—especially those a year or two older—were pressuring them into sexual affairs.

Out of this discussion came the following ways to say no—all thought up by the students themselves:

"There's a lot more to love and a relationship than sex."

"Sex is not the ultimate proof of my love for you."

"What will this do to the rest of our relationship?"

"What will fear of pregnancy do to our relationship?"

"My religion forbids premarital sex."

It is common, I am told, for dating relationships to turn into sexual liaisons largely because it seems the line of least resistance. The 10-week seminar appeared to make the students more thoughtful.

The federal government is today reaching out with varied programs to educate sexually active boys.

"Health, Education and Welfare is becoming bolder about teen contraception," said a San Francisco official of the department. HEW has contributed toward the Population Institute's first mass-media contraception effort, "The Sports Project," which will enlist professional athletes, through broadcast and print-media public-service advertising, to get young boys thinking seriously of the consequences of their sexual activity.

Rochester, New York, has inaugurated a program called MAN, aimed at getting young males into the habit of equalizing responsibility for sex. The *M* in MAN stands for male, the *A* for adolescent, and the *N* for needs. Rochester is presenting MAN as a conference and 12-week discussion seminar.

Since 1970, Planned Parenthood and public health clinics have answered the questions of 400 percent more young people worried about pregnancy than ever before. Boys are appearing in far larger numbers at these clinics, especially at those with adolescent units. They come as half of a couple or in special male groups for boys who become bored with "too much women stuff." Some report problems in being able to get contraception. Over half the boys in one study reported that "sexually active teenagers have a harder time getting birth control items than do adults."

"Teenagers should be allowed to get contraceptives whenever they want them," wrote a ninth-grader in a school government class.

In an HEW pamphlet entitled "Man of Today—the Man Who Cares" (see Resource Guide), some profound questions have been posed for boys willing to consider them:

*"Do you share in choosing and using birth control
. . . assume responsibility for a male method or support
your partner in following through on a female method?*

*"Are you straight about your feelings and avoid
using such pressure lines as 'If you really love me, you'll
cooperate' or 'Just this once' or 'You're just a tease; first
you get me excited and then you back off' or 'You're sexually inhibited, that's what's wrong with you.'*

*"Do you realize that it's a lot cheaper and much
less of a hassle to prevent a baby than to have and care
for one?"*

I recommend that parents and youth-serving agencies
give young men the chance to read this pamphlet. It is
clear from their own statements, their own appalling
revelations of ignorance and lack of formulated values,
that teenagers, as Dr. Sadja Goldsmith, pioneer in San
Francisco adolescent clinics says, want more than pills
and condoms. They want services with affirmative, youth-
oriented approaches, opportunities for counseling, and
answered questions about sex. Boys are especially confused and uneasy about their obligations, the image they
cast, the things they want for themselves. They struggle to
live up to society's image of them as the dominant partner
in sexual relationships, but the truth is that this is not
always so. In a recent television appearance by a number
of high-school students from the Falls Church, Virginia,
human sexuality program, Karen S. told the whole
metropolitan area that it was she who was teaching sexual
facts to her boyfriend.

"He didn't have a sex education class and I've told
him lots of things he didn't know," said Karen.

Her teacher suggested that the young man in question be told that his information gap was to be publicly

aired before the tape of the show was released. Karen agreed and reported later that he had only shaken his head and said, "Well, I *didn't* know, and you *did* tell me."

Such mutual communication, achieved before any crisis, is an essential building block toward a happy, guilt-free relationship.

Our sons will get the information one way or another. It is up to us to see that they get it as straight as this young man did. We cannot afford to stand anxiously by, fearing to offer unwelcome, alienating advice on sensitive matters. We cannot afford to watch passively as our sons take chances and go out into the world untutored.

I believe that this leaves parents obligated to use all possible opportunities to make clear the serious hazards of teenage parenthood, which usually reduces life's options for both young parents and their child. The few who have "made it" and overcome some of the handicaps of early childbearing required wise family and community support. The impact on the girl is always more evident, and this has tended to shield sons from the sense of responsibility that parents can instill early. Young men must be helped to realize that, as a public health leader warns, "to reproduce beyond their capacity to care for a child is to practice aggression against themselves, their family and society."

6

It Happened: Decisions, Decisions

"Let's listen to some records at my house tonight," the gawky boy whispers to the shiny-haired girl in the school corridor. "My parents won't be there."

A few hours later they are in each other's arms in his cluttered bedroom. He is urging her to listen to the promptings of her body. There is no real moment of decision. They are simply swept along because it all seems so right and natural.

Six weeks later she realizes with a sick feeling that she is 15, a high school sophomore, a cheerleader, Daddy's girl—and pregnant.

No parents of teenage girls today can afford to sit back smugly assuming that such scenarios are somebody else's problem. We have already reviewed the statistics, but here are a few more. One girl in four has a baby before the age of 20. Half of these babies are born out of wedlock and many are born after forced marriages. Three out of ten teenagers who have premarital intercourse end up pregnant. With more than half of today's adolescents experimenting sexually, the girl who gets caught could be yours.

Try for a moment to imagine how a girl in her early teens would feel upon hearing or even suspecting that she is pregnant. Suddenly her relatively carefree adolescent world becomes one to which she has forfeited her passport. She is carrying not only a baby, but often a crushing burden of guilt. Her body is struggling to cope with the disturbing change in her glands; her boyfriend is often gone from the picture. I've already quoted the chilling statistic that every ninth young woman who finds herself trapped like this tries to commit suicide. It is not difficult to see why.

As hard as it may be for you as a parent to hear the words, "I'm pregnant," be glad that your daughter is willing to confide in this moment of terrible distress. Try to imagine her bewilderment and fear. Her problems seem overwhelming. She is stunned by her narrowed options.

She desperately needs your help and understanding. "There is no greater compliment a daughter can pay than to confide in her mother or father if she fears she is pregnant," says Dr. Ralph Gause, former director of the first Adolescent Clinic in New York City's Roosevelt Hospital. His conviction deepened with his participation in sex-education-oriented programs in Vermont and in Public Health-oriented pre-natal and post-natal care programs in Mississippi. Upon the parents' basic support can depend the successful management of this crisis.

As a parent, how you react to the news is of crucial importance. You are likely to be overwhelmed with panic, anger, shame at "what the neighbors will think." It is very important to keep in mind in this moment of extreme stress that whatever has happened, this is your daughter and she badly needs your support.

Remember that at this crucial moment your distraught teenager could walk right out of your life. In a surprising number of cases, young women do just that—not because they are ordered from the house but because communication has become impossible. The girl already has too much to bear. A major emotional explosion within the family could be the last straw.

Now that she has broken the news, what is she going to do? How can you help?

A parent's first job is to ensure that a daughter gets medical confirmation of her condition. Urge her gently but firmly to get a pregnancy diagnosis at once. It just *could* be a false alarm. She is at a time of life when menstruation is far from regular, and she is emotionally upset—this in itself could affect her endocrine system. She *has* missed a period, but that can happen without indicating pregnancy. About 30 percent of adolescents who go to a pregnancy detection clinic learn they have been unnecessarily worried. Try to establish whether there are any other signposts pointing toward pregnancy—unusual fatigue, sensitive and swelling breasts, unexplained vomiting.

The symptoms vary tremendously, but with a missed period and her admission that pregnancy *is* a possibility, it is important to help your daughter act quickly. Many parents and daughters prefer to hide their heads in the sand. Denial as a psychological defense is far more common than most of us imagine. Public health nurses have seen again and again the look of utter disbelief on the faces of adolescent girls as much as five months pregnant. Parents, too, can look the other way out of fear of facing facts.

Remind yourself that where pregnancy is involved, nothing is improved by delay. Worse, procrastination will seriously limit a young woman's options.

Where should she go for diagnosis? If she feels comfortable about consulting the family doctor, that is one solution. Until recently, this would have been her *only* medical option, but today young women can choose the privacy of a clinic if they prefer. Planned Parenthood and other medical centers in many cities offer pregnancy diagnosis, including testing, pelvic examination, and counseling. These centers charge as little as $5 and that only to those who can afford to pay. They are funded privately and do not advertise, but in Baltimore, Washington, D.C., Seattle, Philadelphia, and other cities over the country, they stand ready to help confused and worried youngsters. If you don't know your local center, call the Department of Public Health. These centers are easy to work with—most, like the Planned Parenthood Center in Tucson, do not require an appointment for a pregnancy diagnosis, although you must call to find out testing times.

What does testing involve? The young woman should know the date of the first day of her last menstrual period and must bring a clean jar with a sample of her first morning urine. The subsequent wait is usually about a half hour and during this time a social worker will discuss the girl's problems as she sees them in relation to the social-health history. No testing can be done until nine days after the missed period should have begun.

Among worried women seeking pregnancy tests, at least 30 percent are not found to be pregnant, and I have seen some very grateful girls receive the news. "Thank God," one young girl kept saying over and over, tears in her eyes. "Thank God."

Pregnant or not, she hears the diagnosis from the social worker with whom she had the initial interview and is presented with her options. If she is not pregnant, very often, having suffered such a scare, she requests birth control information. Many girls are now choosing the diaphragm; in such a case the girl will come back four weeks after the initial fitting to make certain that she is inserting it correctly. A choice of other safe and reliable methods are also offered.

What about the early pregnancy tests on sale in most drugstores? They are currently under surveillance by the U.S. Food and Drug Administration. All manufacturers of the kits have been requested by the FDA to supply information concerning effectiveness of the kits when used by lay persons. Available information indicates the users can obtain accurate results. Dr. Albert Kolbye, Associate Director for Sciences of the FDA's Bureau of Foods, reports that the FDA is conscious of potential problems with false-negative and false-positive results and is continuing to monitor the situation.

The kits, which sell in the neighborhood of $10, consist of a test tube containing re-agent chemicals, a plastic vial containing purified water, an eye dropper, and a clear plastic holder with mirror to enable you to see the result without touching the box. Complete instructions for use are included.

These do-it-yourself kits have the advantage of complete secrecy, but they do not, like the centers, offer a complete diagnosis or skilled analysis. Some tragic mistakes could ensue. Another advantage of professional diagnosis is that an adolescent who has thought for some days that she is pregnant and finds at last she is not is particularly receptive to advice on how to avoid repeating the nightmare.

If the pregnancy diagnosis is positive, the teenager and her family will be faced with some difficult choices. Will she have the baby or end the pregnancy? If she decides to have the baby, should she keep it or not?

Remember that legally all basic decisions here must ultimately be the teenager's own. This reality is a heavy burden for any parent to face. Naturally a pregnant 13-year-old's needs may differ from those of a 16-year-old, but age is not so dominant a factor in determining the amount and quality of guidance as the adolescent's own experience in decision-making, her maturity, her independence, and her ability to understand the consequences of her choice after having been presented with all the alternatives. A clear expression of how much responsibility a parent is able or willing to assume in helping her carry out her decision may influence a daughter's ultimate choice. A trained professional may offer assistance in objective exploration, helping even the most immature girl accept her own responsibilities.

Just as important as factual information at this point is emotional support. Give her as much of this within the family as possible. She was anxious enough when she suspected pregnancy. Try to imagine how she must feel now that her suspicions have been confirmed. Consider the weight of the decisions that press on her, decisions that are as overpowering as any she will ever have to make. More than 80 percent of the young girls who find themselves in this situation are unmarried and facing pretty much alone the results of a few fleeting moments. A married woman who finds herself with an unplanned pregnancy may experience emotional trauma, but at least she may be bolstered by the support of her husband, her doctor, and the law, which will see to it that the baby has a name, support, and rights of inheritance.

If your daughter turned to you of her own accord upon suspecting she was pregnant, this means you have a solid relationship to build on and you must be careful not to destroy it now. If she has waited until this point to break the news, you must try doubly hard to earn her trust.

The key word as you face the facts together is *sharing*. Let her know that you understand how people can make such mistakes. Empathy is better than sympathy. There is probably never a time in her life when she will need your love more.

Reach out to her not only with words but with physical contact. Look at her, establish eye contact, touch her, use all the small signs that humans who care about each other employ. Reach across that bridge between you and let her know how much she matters to you.

Then, and only then, can you begin to explore options.

Has she told you who is the father of her child? His future role in the situation may or may not turn out to be important, but in any case he must be seriously considered. It is a good idea to inquire tactfully if she has discussed the pregnancy with him.

Who is going to tell her own father? Because of the special relationship that exists between most fathers and daughters, he may have an even harder time with the news than you did. Almost every father unconsciously carries an image of his daughter as an eternally innocent girl. The decision on how to break the news depends on what kind of a man he is. You and your daughter may well decide that he will need some preparing. As with everything else at this moment, the ultimate decision must be hers; you will only present options.

Don't expect your husband to be calm. He will

probably blame himself a little. "How have I failed?" is a common reaction. He will wonder if there is any way he could have prevented this. Be prepared for an emotional explosion. If you anticipate one, it might be that you should get your daughter's permission to break the news alone. If he is apt to make a scene, don't let him confront her until he has begun to make some adjustment, is beginning to accept what has happened.

What about brothers and sisters? If they are mature teens, it may make it easier for the family as a whole if they are told at the start. They are after all, part of the same generation, and may be able to act as a bridge between you and your daughter. This could be important. If they are younger, it is probably better not to tell them until decisions have been made.

Avoid at all costs the knee-jerk reaction that she must marry the boy. Almost 85 percent of the families of unwed pregnant girls think first of urging marriage. This is not a solution, merely wishful thinking. Marriages made like this are wide open for divorce. Your daughter is nearly four times as likely to end up divorced if she marries this boy now. Many pregnancies before marriage are the result of casual experimentation. An amazing number of young girls who become accidentally pregnant don't want to marry the father.

"I knew all along I shouldn't have married him," said a girl whose marriage lasted exactly one year after a forced wedding. "I just couldn't think of anything else to do."

Discuss honestly with your teenager whether she is ready to be a mother. In a scant week or two she has passed from being a child to being a prospective parent, and she has scarcely had time to consider what it means. Would she be ready to give up the freedom of doing what she wants to do when she wants to do it? Give up prom dresses, dates, all the trappings of adolescence? Does she realize that bringing a child into this world means she will devote at least 18 years, longer than she has lived, to caring for this baby at the expense of her own personal life? Is she ready to be a responsible mother?

Explore with her where she and the baby would live. If she brings the infant home for her family to help care for, has she considered the Pandora's box of emotional conflict this may open? Is it a fair financial burden to impose on her parents, her brothers and sisters? Has she considered whether her parents are still young enough to rise above the noise and confusion inevitably attendant on the bringing up of a tiny child? Conversely, would the baby perhaps be welcomed into an extended family that includes a grandmother longing to do useful work, loving brothers and sisters who would delight in the baby and compete for a chance to help take care of it?

Your daughter could, of course, keep the baby and set herself up alone. She is entitled to public assistance, no matter what her parents' financial position, if she is what the welfare agencies call "emancipated"—maintaining her own household. Seventy percent of adolescent pregnancies are out of wedlock and all but 10 percent (who probably don't apply) of the young mothers receive welfare allowances. There are grim realities involved here. Aid to Families with Dependent Children pays assistance for the child and mother, but this is usually enough only for survival at bare subsistence level. Does your daughter know how to handle a budget, how to take care of a baby alone? Does she have the inner resources to live essentially by herself? A tiny baby can be disappointing company—it often is, as many of these children have found out, "just boring." As the child grows out of infancy, there will be even more demands, sometimes irritating.

In spite of the discouraging realities of too-early

motherhood, today 90 percent of teenage mothers who are not married keep their babies. "Kids with kids" is the trend, partly because of a more permissive philosophy and partly because it is the thing, like wearing jeans, frizzing your hair, loving Elton John. It is part of the legacy of the flower children who urged the celebration of the natural life. Rock music also urges it, and so do all the mother's instincts, now currently in tune with the mode. "I Wanna Have Your Baby" is a big hit. Much of teenage intercourse takes place to the hypnotic rhythms of rock music.

And then there is that other heartrending reason why young people are keeping their babies—for companionship. Social workers call this the "baby-doll syndrome" and many a complex reason for failure to avoid pregnancy is laid at its door. In the dolly syndrome, the mother-to-be has fantasies of an all-loving infant, a small human that she can call her own. It is common among both the impoverished and the emotionally deprived.

These are only some of the reasons why children keep their children. Each child-mother's reasons are an individual blend. Many even believe that pregnancy gives them status among their peers and the adult world.

 What about adoption?

If your daughter decides to give up the baby, she will find the process quite different today from what it once was. The natural mother of an adopted child is given far more information about prospective adoptive parents than in her mother's day—the chances are that she will be allowed to suggest the type of adoptive parents from several files presented to her. Agencies, as always, will make every effort to match child and new parents. A young mother is no longer relinquishing her baby to a faceless stranger, and she is informed that the child at 18 may in some states be given complete information about its biological mother's background. The process of adoption today is far more one in which she participates than something that happens to her.

Jean Colwell, a teacher in the Young Parents' Program in a California school district, has on file a touching letter written by a 17-year-old mother to the parents who were selected from many well-investigated applicants.

"Hello," she wrote (how do you address the people to whom you have given your baby?),

I want you to know I really love my baby. But you two can give him so much more than I ever could at my age.

I want you to know that I don't think of myself as the mother in the full sense of the word . . . I did carry him for nine months and gave birth to him, but it seems to me that the hardest part of parents is from the time the child is an infant until he reaches maturity . . . The time the child is in the womb is the easiest time the mother will ever know. Parenting is probably the hardest job on the face of the earth, and it's the one least taught. In my opinion, people take it too lightly. Maybe it's because they don't want to accept the fact that it's that important or that hard.

When he's older, tell him his mother loved him enough to give him up.

In considering adoption with your daughter, remember the importance of preserving her freedom of choice. It is hard not to be influenced by professional counselors, all of whom have different predispositions while trying their best to be nonjudgmental. If your daughter consults agencies concerned with offering contraceptives, they may send out unconscious messages to terminate the pregnancy. If she talks with personnel at some religious adoption agencies, the scales may subliminally tip toward adoption. Whoever advises her professionally should be —and undoubtedly strives to be—as unbiased as possible, strong enough to leave the decision to her, hard though it may be. Her right to choose must be preserved at all costs, but bias may surface in subtle ways. There are code words, key phrases like "for the best interests of the child." Even the attitude of medical personnel can influence a young girl as much as words.

Other bias closer to her will influence her. Seventy percent of the young fathers, it is estimated, don't want the child given up. Sometimes they make promises that sway the mother, promises they later cannot keep.

"I'm responsible," said the young boyfriend of a girl whom he feared might become a mother. "I'll marry her and take care of them both."

"Has she had the pregnancy test yet?" the counselor wanted to know.

"No. I haven't got the money."

Should a pregnant teenager decide to release her baby for adoption, there are various private agencies as well as residential maternity homes like the Salvation Army that will help. State laws prevail, but it is important to go to established agencies and avoid private arrangements between doctors and lawyers, some of whom may unethically offer money and free services in exchange for the baby. Despite years of attempts to combat it, this illegal practice persists and young mothers still become involved in black-market deals. Federal legislation to protect the mother, baby, and the adoptive parents has so far failed to get through Congress, and young mothers without guidance are still trapped in shady arrangements.

A directory of qualified adoption agencies in every state is available from the Child Welfare League of America (see Resource Guide). The teen dealing with a reputable agency will surrender her baby by proper legal process, important in avoiding the heartbreak of quasi-legal arrangements which can go awry.

What about the rights of unwed fathers?

Judges and lawyers are bound by a 1975 Supreme Court decision to secure the father's consent to surrender the child for adoption, even to the extent of trying to identify and locate him if he is no longer in the picture in order to fulfill the legal requirements.

Many adoption agencies agree with this principle but find it hard to execute. The mother may refuse to give the father's name or may say she doesn't know in order to avoid the complications of having him step forward and claim his child. This happens infrequently, in which case the judge must decide with the help of the agency's findings what is "the best interest of the child." In practice, producing convincing evidence for the judge that every effort has been made to apprise the father of his rights may cause expense and critical delay in cases in which it has been necessary to locate a father who does not wish to be involved.

When adoption is being considered as an alternative, it is important to make the decision as early as possible and to apprise the father of his legal rights and responsibility. It can be especially damaging when the young couple makes a wait-and-see decision and later has to give up the baby. The mother in this predicament may be loaded with guilt as the baby gets older. A 3-year-old child often is scarred by a feeling that all relationships are a sometime thing, whereas a baby placed in a home at birth undergoes no such trauma. The adoptive parents suffer an additional burden of adjustment when adoption occurs late.

Placement experts say that today an adoptable baby is at a premium and will always be placed in a good home. "Our affiliated agencies countrywide have announced that a four to five year waiting period can be anticipated by an approved couple," says Emily Gardiner, information consultant of the Child Welfare League of America.

Perhaps the young girl will keep the baby or perhaps she will give it up. But no matter which option she follows, there is bound to be some degree of guilt. If she keeps the baby, she may worry that she should have given it up. If she gives it up, she may feel she has abandoned it. If she marries the father, it could be from a sense of duty, could seriously limit her future. If she strikes out on her own, she faces the specters of loneliness and almost certain poverty.

It is now, at the very moment when she seems to have broken her parents' hearts, that she most needs their love and affection. Wrapped in her troubles, bewildered by swift retribution for an act that seemed so natural, she does not know where to turn. She still must break the news to her peers, her teachers, the others who touch her life. If normal adolescence is a no-man's-land, imagine what it is to be adolescent and pregnant. She is cast for a role for which she is not ready, and there is no way out.

Unless she should decide on abortion.

7

The Abortion Option

"Decisions are the hardest part about being pregnant," confides 16-year-old Maria to the school counselor. She looks at her chunky shoes and then at the ceiling. "My boyfriend doesn't want me to have an abortion and that makes it harder. Sometimes I do and sometimes I don't. I just don't know what to do."

The counselor nods. Many of the young people seeking her help have conflicting feelings.

"Just remember that the decisions are yours," she says quietly. "There *are* choices and what you have to decide is what you really want. Perhaps talking it over with your mother would help. You might be surprised how much she will understand."

Whether or not to terminate a pregnancy is a hard decision for any woman. It is an especially difficult choice for a young woman who lacks experience in the world. Opting for abortion often involves a ruthless shattering of romantic fantasies, the intrusions of the grimmest kind of reality into an unformed view of life.

Says a well-known Washington director of an abortion clinic, a gynecologist who is also a psychiatrist:

"There is always . . . sorrow in [the termination of a pregnancy]; for that there is little we can do. Sometimes the sorrow is conscious and sometimes it's subconscious and doesn't come out until later in therapy. We try to give the girls we see all the emotional support that we can. There is grief for each loss of a part of the body. It is a terrible thing to lose part of yourself. We see it in all sorts of ways, loss of teeth, loss of hair. If you don't grieve, the grief can surface later in bizarre ways such as another pregnancy. We see many repeats here."

It is not easy for a teenager to choose abortion, but neither is it easy to continue the pregnancy. Abortion may loom stark and frightening to a young girl, but many times it brings not only a profound sense of relief, but even unexpected psychological benefits. Often, though not always, it matures an adolescent who has for the first time in her life faced the difficulty of making an important decision alone and going through with it. More than a few teenagers have emerged from a pregnancy termination with a stronger sense of self, fortified with the knowledge that they have faced and dealt with one of the most demanding moments of their lives.

Patty, a 16-year-old in a large ghetto area, was one of these girls. She discovered that she was pregnant only a year after her unwed younger sister had borne a child which the hard-pressed family had absorbed. Determined to put no further burdens on her parents, Patty came alone to Planned Parenthood asking for help. She told agency workers that she wanted an abortion and wanted it kept secret.

This young woman developed from the experience into a more mature and responsible person. She became a peer counselor with special empathy for other young girls going through what she herself had good reason to understand. Personnel at the agency watched with respect as she grew into a self-assured, compassionate, thoughtful adult.

Patty met disaster and made an opportunity of it. Sometimes, however, things don't work out quite so easily. What can parents do to help their daughters through this trying period of choice?

The first thing they can do is listen. Many girls have never had the chance to really talk the problem out. Verbalizing their conflicting feelings can help them find out what they really want. Discussions like this provide an opportunity for parents to help their daughters understand the choices involved. Professionals say it is usually the girl who has not clearly understood her options who suffers the worst trauma.

The choice, however, must remain with the girl herself and she must be clear about this. Legally, the decision at any age is her responsibility and it would be a mistake for parents not to recognize this. In a 1976 opinion, the Supreme Court emphatically declared that, "Constitutional rights do not mature and come into being magically only when one attains the state-defined age of majority." (*Planned Parenthood* v. *Danforth*). If she opts for an abortion, the parents' role will be to ensure that it is done legally, by a competent physician. Parents must also make every effort to see that, once their daughter has made a choice of abortion, it is done as soon as humanly possible.

In offering daughters support during this trying time, parents may well wish they had a shoulder of their own to lean on. They do, and they can find it any number of places—the family doctor, the nondenominational Clergy Counseling Service, or Planned Parenthood clinics. If the situation has really made deep scars, they might want to visit a community mental health service clinic. In most cases, specialists seem to feel that this consulting is best done when daughters are not present. Most clinics also find that it is better to work out the problems of parents through a different staff member than the one working with the daughter. Only after parents have come to grips with the problem themselves can they help their confused young daughter stick to whatever decision she makes and learn that, no matter what has happened, the important thing is to get on with life.

It is also important to remind a daughter at this moment of decision that interrupting an unwanted pregnancy now does not mean that she cannot become the happy mother of a wanted child at some future time. There is no scientific evidence that having an abortion affects a later pregnancy. At the right time, under the right circumstances, pregnancy can be an ultimate fulfillment and your daughter should know this. A joyless pregnancy can leave more of a scar on the mother—and thus often on the child—than an abortion. Dr. Takey Crist, director of the Crist Clinic for Women, who sees over 100 teen-agers a month in his oby/gyn service, puts it this way:

"Any girl who becomes pregnant before she is physically capable, emotionally ready and able to cope with the complex job of rearing a baby is in an extremely difficult situation, particularly if she is in the younger end of the age spectrum."

The choice of abortion depends on many things—

alternatives for taking care of the child, the young girl's beliefs about life, her religion, and perhaps the feelings of others important to her. It is often helpful for a pregnant teenager to discuss abortion options with someone besides her immediate family, someone she trusts. Sometimes this helps to reassure her that the decision she will make is one she can live with.

Some adolescents reject abortion for a cluster of reasons that add up to psychological revulsion.

"I just couldn't, I just couldn't," said Karen over and over again. "It just doesn't seem right." Echoes of tradition, threads of the past deep in the subconscious, a vague determination to live in tune with the current emphasis on "the right to life" or following nature's way in spite of the complex demands of society sometimes persuade a teenage girl that she should bear the child. If she feels this way, these feelings must be respected—again, the very important choice is hers alone. Old enough to be pregnant is old enough to make this decision, no matter how hard this is on those around her.

Counselors in clinics often see teens who have been pushed into terminating a pregnancy which they, consciously or subconsciously, did not want to end but agreed to because of overprotective and anxious parents. We can learn a lot from the case of Sheila, a 16-year-old who visited a counselor in an abortion clinic with her parents.

Sheila sat, silent and submissive, beside her mother and father as arrangements for an abortion went forward. But during a preliminary history-taking session that opened the door to intimate problems, a sympathetic caseworker drew from the girl the tragic story of the death of the boy Sheila had expected to marry. He had been killed in a freak high-tension-wire accident and she was convinced that having his baby would keep something of him alive. Counselors subsequently talked to her parents, gradually making it clear to them that their daughter was accepting abortion against her wishes. Two weeks later, after exploring every possible alternative with her parents and the counselor, Sheila decided to have the abortion, but with a mind now fully convinced that it was what the dead boy himself would have wanted had he lived.

If a young girl chooses to terminate her pregnancy, her parents should be certain that she receives the care her emotional and physical health demands. Every county medical society has a roster of competent doctors and lists affiliates with 600 nationwide clinics. State or county maternal or child health clinics or comprehensive adolescent clinics can be located through the state departments of health or welfare. United Way and Community Chest organizations in many cities have information and referral services, including hospitals and qualified women's clinics prepared to provide in-patient or out-patient abortion.

Of special interest is a pilot counseling center, Catholic Alternatives, recently founded by Catholic laity in New York City. This is an educational organization offering as many alternatives as possible in problems of responsible sexuality. It aims to encourage informed choices tuned to individual conscience. Its literature describes it as intending "to counsel teenagers, parents, grandparents and all other humans." This group may provide a unique source for Catholic parents or others seeking help with a son or daughter's problems.

Joan Harriman, the president and executive director of Catholic Alternatives, believes that abortion can be greatly reduced by proper use of birth control methods. The primary goal, she says, is to educate those who need it, particularly teenagers. "We support women in their choice to terminate a pregnancy in accordance with their medical, psychological, and economic capacities," she states. "While we do not advocate abortion, we do support the Supreme Court ruling that the decision should be made by each woman and her doctor."

Catholic Alternatives plans a nationwide outreach which is presently being developed in various cities. Seminars and workshops dealing with religion and reproduction will be offered. As part of this attempt to reach the public, the group is currently developing educational materials. Special emphasis is being given to teens as peer counselors, lecturers at sexual responsibility sessions, and members of the editorial staff of "What Is It?" an innovative sex education newsletter by teens for teens. Out of school hours, young people also help maintain a Teen Hotline.

Many of the clinics that provide abortions offer ancillary services such as pregnancy testing, contraceptive advice, pre- and post-natal services, and counseling. If the teenager lives in a small community where there is no such clinic or services, there will never be a better time to spend what money is available to go where the best facilities are. In fact, going to a clinic or doctor outside her hometown may make her feel more secure.

Visiting a clinic is not signing a contract to terminate the pregnancy. The real decision will be made after a consultation with the staff. Boyfriends often go along on these visits; a close friend or a parent can also be a big help.

The majority of abortion clinics have very little in common with formal hospital atmosphere. They are generally staffed with people who, from the making of the first appointment until the end of the final visit, seem to care. The receptionist, the nurse, the counselor, and the doctor are trained to convey all information in a nonjudgmental, nonthreatening manner. They look at each girl as an individual. An appointment usually should be made for the first talk. Visitors to such clinics will be encouraged by the supportive, friendly way clinic social workers take the initial call, securing precise information from the patient, explaining clinic regulations, and preparing young callers for their initial visit.

No effort is spared to make these centers attractive. Sterile waiting rooms, brusque nurses, endless waits which raise misgivings all over again are seldom part of the picture. Most clinics have extra volunteer counselors especially trained to make the young girl feel at ease, many of them young people who have had abortions themselves. They are always willing to take time to answer questions, several times, as is often necessary, in groups or alone, ironing out fears and reassuring when doubts crop up. Members of the staff are always prepared to discuss the procedure, postoperative care, and subsequent contraception.

Teenagers and their parents should be prepared for certain groups which sometimes stand outside abortion centers to try to influence girls and their families with false depictions of the abortion process, photographs of mutilated fetuses, and the like. It is important to remember, whatever one's personal view of abortion, that the procedure is simple, safe—probably the most common operation done today in this country—and absolutely an individual right.

Things have changed since that day during the Depression when I saw Mary dying in her blood-stained bed. Most parents today can remember when women wanting to terminate a pregnancy were forced to risk their lives with self-induced or nonmedical procedures. Before abortion was legalized in the U.S., pregnancies were often terminated under appalling conditions.

On January 22, 1973, the Supreme Court legalized abortion, basing the decision on the Fourteenth Amendment, guaranteeing the right to privacy. As a result of this decision, the choice of abortion rests entirely on a woman and her physician. No state law may interfere in this personal decision before the thirteenth week. In the second three months, the state may require that the abortion be performed under optimum conditions for maternal health by qualified doctors. After twenty-four weeks of gestation, during the period of potential viability of the fetus, abortion is forbidden except when the life or health of the mother is threatened. Doctors act in accordance with these specific limitations.

Abortion procedures will differ according to the period of gestation. One rule that applies to all abortion is: The earlier, the safer. Dr. Willard Cates, Jr., of the U.S. Center for Disease Control, underscores the benefit of performing any type of abortion without delay as soon as pregnancy is diagnosed, especially in the case of teenagers. Early abortions are remarkably safe, with less than 1 complication in 200—but a delay of even 1 week is enough to affect the relative safety.

What are the currently acceptable abortion procedures and what do they involve?

Dr. Takey Crist describes them as follows: In most states, if the mother-to-be is no more than 12 weeks pregnant, suction curettage is the most frequently used procedure to terminate a pregnancy. This involves the dilation of the mouth of the womb, the insertion of a very small tube, and the removal of fetus and placenta by means of a vacuum pump under the most sterile conditions. Anesthesia can be either local or spinal, and the procedure will take only about three minutes. The bluntness of the instruments and the mechanics of aspirating the uterine contents make this procedure an extremely safe one.

The D&C (dilation and curettage) is another method widely used during early pregnancy. The cervix is widened by the insertion of a metal dilator and the lining of the uterus is scraped out with a curved blade called a curette. The procedure, done under general anesthesia, may take anywhere from five to ten minutes and requires, sometimes, a day's hospitalization. It is a simple, harmless, standard medical procedure that will not affect future health or fertility.

Some states permit clinics to do abortions between 12 and 16 weeks by suction. In states where this is not permissible, or when the doctor thinks that the pregnancy has gone beyond the safe time for termination by this method, the salt procedure will be used. It is usually the choice after 16 weeks and involves the replacement of the fluid inside the uterine cavity with a hypertonic salt or sugar solution. As a result, the woman goes into labor and expels all the contents within 18–36 hours. This procedure may be psychologically difficult since sometimes it involves days of waiting in the hospital before the fetus is delivered.

Dr. Crist also reports that research is now underway on other methods of terminating a pregnancy with the use of special drugs. Prostaglandins, which act to stimulate muscular contractions and cause the uterus to expel its contents, are now approved.

A recovery room of an abortion clinic is today apt

to be full of young couples or girls accompanied by their mothers, even though many middle-aged parents of the girls involved cannot bring themselves to accept what their children face as an accepted part of life. Every shade of acceptance and denial sooner or later finds its way into a typical abortion clinic, and what goes on in the recovery room and thereafter has a great deal to do with how the young girl will look on her parents later.

It is important to remember that what parents feel, and let their daughter know they feel, about what happens to her in an abortion clinic can affect her acceptance of her own sexuality. If the girl's mother has trouble adjusting, the relationship between mother and daughter may be damaged. The young girls waiting out the hour after the abortion are, whether or not they know it or feel it at the time, in a crucial and vulnerable moment of their lives. The most brittle of them has suffered some loss, and all have experienced glandular changes. It is a time for reassurance of unaltered parental love.

Many parents are uneasy at allowing an adolescent unmarried daughter to receive birth control information at this time. Some feel that giving permission for her to have such instruction is equivalent to saying, "Go ahead, do what you want." The plain truth is that a young girl who has been sexually active will probably remain that way. No studies have ever shown that the availability of contraceptives encourages promiscuous behavior. Keeping young people ignorant and uninformed can lead only to more tragedy.

Girls in abortion clinics often claim that they won't need contraceptive information because they have learned their lesson and will never see the boy again. Some go further, vowing they're never going to have intercourse again. These statements are obviously unrealistic. Prevention is a lot better than cure. Parents who find it hard to accept this, or to discuss their feelings about their children's sexuality, might want to take part in a discussion group with the clinic counselors. Or they might want to make an appointment with the doctor or staff member who has shown interest in their daughter's problems (most such conferences are free). It often helps to talk things out with a sympathetic person to whom your problems are not new. Again, as mentioned earlier, if truly deep scars have resulted from your daughter's unexpected pregnancy, the community health clinic may help to work out any remaining inability to deal with the way things are by getting professional treatment.

With all the decisions made, the emotional problems faced, it is time to think about financial matters.

How much does it cost when a teenager opts for abortion?

A suction curettage during the first 12 weeks of pregnancy usually costs from $150 to $250, depending on locality and clinic policy. The more complex and expensive hospital procedure of the second trimester ranges from $500 to $800, according to circumstances and the physical response of the girl. These prices are the average rate. They can seem astronomically high to the girl without ready funds.

It is sometimes possible to get free abortions in private clinics. Many more will work out time payments and often have such resources as lines to privately funded institutions that will help pay. Planned Parenthood may know of discretionary funds. Public welfare may be able to refer the girl to voluntary or church agencies with money earmarked for these situations.

Ironically, at a time when a clear majority of Americans favor legalized abortion (a 1977 Gallup Poll found that 3 out of 4 Americans approved legal abortion before the last trimester), Congress and many state legislatures are considering various types of anti-abortion legislation. These could restrict the availability of safe abortion care by cutting off public funds, curtailing the rights of minors, or banning all abortion by an amendment to the Constitution defining life as beginning with conception. Of particular concern is the Hyde Amendment, which put an end to federally-funded Medicaid abortions, implicitly robbing part of the population of the right *not* to bear a child.

Some states, however, fund abortions for the poor and those receiving welfare assistance. In the two years since the adoption of the Hyde Amendment in 1977, certain states have assumed payment for abortion and each of these has an established policy. (Names of these states and the requirements for eligibility are summarized at the end of the Resource Guide.) The District of Columbia, which still voluntarily pays for abortions, records more abortions than births, one-third of the former performed on teenagers. At present, however, to get funding in most states, you will have to prove that carrying the child to term would endanger the life of the mother, or that the pregnancy is the result of rape or incest.

Backers of the Hyde Amendment might reflect on the fact that a lack of money usually means more than that the parents cannot pay for an abortion for an accidentally pregnant teenage daughter. Most families living on the thin edge of solvency are handicapped by their environment, their large families, and the often self-destructive values fostered by their way of life.

Elaine was such a case. She had known Richard for almost two years when, at 15, she became pregnant.

Her instant reaction was to keep the news from her parents. She felt sure they would be too angry to give her any kind of support and, in any case, could do nothing financially to help her.

Although she could not turn to her parents, Richard was determined to see her through. Together they decided that an abortion was the best answer to their trouble. Neither of them knew the first thing about how to go about getting one, but they did find out that there would be money required. Since neither of them had ever possessed more than a dollar or two at a time, Richard went about getting the money in the only way he knew—shoplifting.

He was caught.

I wish I could say that, once the reason for his act became known, an agency was able to help the young people. No one did. Elaine had the baby, adding one more mouth to a desperately poor family household which was already on public welfare assistance.

There are probably many Elaines throughout the country and the endorsement of the Hyde Amendment will work many such hardships. A doctor in North Carolina who sees such cases every day in his work wrote to his senator about this:

Dear Senator:

I saw a patient today named Rosalee.

Her problem, Senator, is that her 17-year-old mentally retarded daughter is pregnant. Her husband is disabled and on welfare.

Before Rosalee can ask me what to do, I know already the doors are closed. What do I tell her, Senator? I am waiting for your answer.

There are no simple answers in abortion. But again I want to stress my own belief that, as parents, we must remember that a decision to terminate a pregnancy is entirely the girl's own. I believe that we, as concerned citizens, must make sure that the abortion option is available as a matter of individual right. All women, whatever their age, should be free to make an informed choice about something which so significantly affects their personal fate.

The key phrase here is responsible choice. As Dr. Crist reminds us: "Society is asking that quality of life be the cornerstone of Western culture. Women of all ages are best served by medical ethics that allow them to choose and make the final decision for themselves. A thirteen-year-old girl, impregnated by her father, can have a legal abortion today and return to school with a maximum chance for normal adolescence. A girl who has contracted German measles can, with an abortion, be spared the doubts based on predictable increase of the chances of deformity. Because of the alternative of abortion, an eighteen-year-old boy would not be forced to marry a fifteen-year-old girl with whom he has little in common and be obliged to quit school, carrying for the rest of his life the burdens evolving from too young fatherhood.

"We encourage nobody to have an abortion. But we cannot stand by to see the mental anguish and physical suffering of those compelled to have a child they do not want."

Consider the words of a 17-year-old girl who wrote to her doctor after an abortion: "Thank you for allowing me to choose the only alternative that was *in my case* possible."

Choice, yes. But we must remember that abortion is never a substitute for an accepted form of birth control.

My experience over the years confirms the need for comprehensive services emphasizing prevention.

It is significant that the proposed regulations for the administration of the 1978 Adolescent Pregnancy Program reflects the legislative intent that all options must be offered to teenagers, including the abortion option. If abortion procedures are not available within the agency serving the adolescent, she must be referred to an appropriate source for this service. The right to the consideration of all alternatives, regardless of age or marital status, is thus confirmed.

8

Planning for the Baby

Abortion is an alternative that never entered the head of 16-year-old Susan, a representative example of the social phenomenon new to many families that finds an adolescent with an unplanned, out-of-wedlock pregnancy living at home with her parents and planning to keep the baby.

Susan's decision to wait out her term in her middle-class home would have been unthinkable ten years ago. Then, she would have been taken overseas for an abortion, banished to out-of-town relatives, or forced to withdraw in shame to the seclusion of an institution.

I remember watching a nun registering a young pregnant girl in an infant and maternal center in Chicago in 1958. "We are here to protect," she told me. "The girl is never registered under her correct name. The police can't touch her here, nor can the FBI."

Such institutions were essentially dormitories in which the young girls were allowed to wait out their term. Recreation consisted of walks within a fenced-in area; the girls were isolated from the world, made to feel that they were being penalized for breaking the laws of society. I remember vividly a newly appointed director of one such home saying to me back in those early days, "I want to change the bleak atmosphere that still surrounds too many maternity homes. We are beginning to build a better recreational and school program for these girls . . . and we need more modern nurseries to care for the babies until adoption procedures are completed. Almost 70 percent of the babies born here last year were hurried off to adoptive parents to hide their mother's shame. Too many people still believe that an unmarried mother is a no-good."

Like so much else, this has vastly changed, though not everywhere. In all probability the home where Susan would go to have her baby today if she did not remain with her parents would be a more enlightened place. New attitudes toward the unwed mother have changed the entire atmosphere of these homes. The young mother-to-be is no longer shrouded in secrecy. She is visited by her friends, she goes to concerts and movies, she lives in a room or dormitory decorated with pictures and posters and other reminders that she is still part of the everyday world. She has a range of opportunities for learning while she is in the home—counseling and guidance, advice on parenting, nutrition, and consumer thrift. She can continue regular schooling and take part in group therapy.

Such homes are usually subsidized by public or private contributions. Payments are related to the family's ability to pay. In the Washington, D.C., Florence Crittenton Program, for example, the fee ranges from

$10 to $28 a day, often augmented by grants or loans. You can find Florence Crittenton Homes in 40 cities, Salvation Army homes in 34. A directory of residential treatment programs relating to single pregnant girls and to young single mothers and their children, provided by the Child Welfare League of America, lists information about 600 institutions and their programs (see Resource Guide).

Today only 5 percent of pregnant unmarried girls take advantage of such homes, and those that do are usually in the young age bracket. A large proportion come from disrupted homes or from families which have rejected them, and many of these institutions have changed their policies to reach the socially or emotionally disturbed girl.

Susan will see no need for their assistance, though. Facing the world pregnant with no visible marital partner is now accepted in Susan's circle. Her friends stand solidly behind her.

Susan's parents, however, do not feel quite the same. Susan and her mother were never particularly close and her father is shattered by what has happened to his young daughter. Both parents, however, have privately sworn to conceal their feelings, especially since the baby's father has disappeared from the scene. Hurt, defensive, and angry in turn, they have closed ranks to protect Susan from the raised eyebrows of their contemporaries and the host of problems that lie in wait for her and for them.

For all her bravado, it's not simple for Susan either. In public she holds her head high. Privately, in the little room she has lived in since she was a baby, she has misgivings about her decision and is bitter about some of the neighbors who are avoiding her either out of disapproval

or embarrassment. Susan is particularly hurt by the attitude of her mother's friend, "Aunt Jane," who doesn't
seem to know where to look when she comes to call and
encounters Susan sprawled on the sofa, obviously pregnant. "How are you coming along with your studies?" she
asks, averting her gaze, and then hurries on as if Susan
had some disease best not mentioned in public.

In spite of such inevitable hurts, there are comforting and caring places and people who can give Susan
and her peers the help, encouragement, and up-to-date
medical assistance needed during pregnancy. Susan's
medical health will be looked after in an out-patient
treatment center, a place where she will feel at home.
Such centers are hospital-based or broad-based com-
munity-sponsored clinics, some with special units for
adolescents. They are usually full of bright, informal
rooms, with comfortable chairs and cushions on the floor
and a supply of well-presented literature on prenatal
checkups, delivery, and baby care. Adolescents, like
older women, want to know what the doctor is doing
from the first examination to delivery and resent being
kept in the dark like a child. These clinics today have
group talks, explicit movies about what to expect in a
breast or pelvic examination, and many have peer counselors as well. Most try to arrange to have the teens see
the same doctors on each visit to avoid the nervousness
new faces are apt to cause in the examining room.

Johns Hopkins Center for School-Age Mothers
and Their Infants in Baltimore is a fine example of a
hospital-based clinic. Its program provides services to
pregnant teens and young mothers—comprehensive care
which extends from the prenatal period to three years
after birth. Besides the obvious medical, nutritional, and
psychosocial care, it also offers well-baby care, develop-

ment screening, family planning services, educational/ vocational counseling, and day care centers. There are linkages with various social and medical agencies of the city.

An outstanding example of a modern broad-based program with comprehensive adolescent pregnancy services is the Delaware Adolescent Program, Inc. (DAPI), which was administered for many years by Dr. Lulu Mae Nix, now Director of the Office of Adolescent Pregnancy Programs for HEW. "DAPI gives the confused pregnant adolescent everything from a good academic education to special courses in labor and delivery, nutrition, sewing, beauty culture, sex education and family living," says Dr. Nix. At DAPI a teen mother-to-be learns how to care for the baby after it arrives. The service even extends to the young fathers, offering social aid for the entire family, and contraceptives are available to those who need and want them. Significantly, very few repeat pregnancies come out of DAPI—8 reported from more than 500 girls. This compares significantly with the 1 girl in 4 in the 15- to 19-year-old age group who, according to national statistics *becomes pregnant again* within a year of giving birth. This clinic has made it clear how important a group of energetic volunteers can be in involving the community and really making a difference to the welfare of the young mothers. Community funds are liberally added to state-federal support of this model comprehensive care program.

Susan did not choose, as she might have, a private doctor for delivery. If your daughter prefers a private obstetrician, it might be best to ask him a few searching questions. Does he have the time to give this young girl the attention her youth demands? Unlike the clinics, with their counseling staff, most physicians would serve her alone, with no backup staff, and adolescents need to be told over and over again answers to their questions. Would he tire of giving such special attention? Can he honestly say that he has no bias toward a young unmarried pregnant girl?

If your daughter chooses a private doctor, you can help her by encouraging her to follow his advice between visits. It is, for instance, particularly important to convince her that she should abandon the junk foods to which young girls of her age are commonly addicted and eat a proper diet that will build a strong body for her baby. Teens generally mean well when it comes to nutrition, but Susan shares her generation's weakness for candy bars, potato chips, pizzas, pop; all the things that always went, in her mind, with TV watching. She has difficulty understanding that the healthy growth of the fetus in utero depends upon proper diet, avoidance of any medicines which have not been prescribed and abstinence from alcoholic beverages.

"Would you feed the baby that?" her mother once asked in exasperation, watching Susan dispose of a bag of munchies washed down with orange pop.

Most especially, Susan's parents are anxious for her to stop smoking. Susan picked up the habit a year or so ago and is apt to light up when she is nervous. The current knowledge that smoking is dangerous to her health doesn't impress her, for she, like the rest of the young, knows she will live forever. Her doctor has had to explain to her the special dangers to her baby if she continues to smoke.

What has lately come to light on this subject is frightening. Reports from NIH's 1979 studies of 50,000 pregnancies in 12 hospitals confirm earlier warnings of dangers to the unborn and newborn. The frequencies of stillbirths or premature births, malformations of the heart or other organs, and increase of the danger of sudden infant crib deaths climb when a pregnant woman smokes. Susan's own health is also adversely affected. Parents who smoke themselves and have decided it would be well to stop may find this is an excellent opportunity to benefit doubly by also setting an example for their daughter.

Susan's parents should also be aware that Susan needs special exercises prior to delivery, since many younger adolescent bodies are ill-prepared for childbirth. Elysa Markowitz, Director of Perinatal Education, Hollywood Presbyterian Medical Center in Los Angeles, reports: "Doctors, in relating their impressions to exercise teachers in several special teen pregnancy programs, have noted a substantial difference between teens who have exercised and those who hadn't. There is a greater ease in delivery when the girl has exercised, especially exercises that focus on the pelvis. If she accepts that part of her body, is familiar with how to move it, has control and the ability to relax and accept the process of labor, she does fine. Those who haven't prepared for the birth may have difficult labors, sometimes ending in a Caesarean birth.

"If the teenager has been encouraged to accept her body with a sense of ease and naturalness, she will also accept the birth process confidently. If her self-image is good, she will be motivated to do what is healthful for her body. If she doesn't think well of herself, she will be less willing to exercise. Discipline is born from desire, not force.

"An affirmative attitude on the part of the pregnant teenager's support people—teachers, parents, peers—can make a big difference. Parents may need to take a look at how they view their own bodies. If they feel there are 'dirty parts,' that gets conveyed. A young woman needs healthy role models upon which to fashion a positive birth experience," Ms. Markowitz concludes.

Susan and her mother can exercise together. Exercise not only benefits middle-aged bodies but provides a nice form of companionship. Adults close to pregnant adolescents must get them to understand that exercise is fun.

Before undertaking any form of exercise, consult your doctor or clinic exercise director and obtain their approval. Teenagers are more prone to miscarriage than older women.

Most clinics understand that adolescent mothers-to-be are locked into a process which frightens them—something that parents should also keep in mind. Early on, most clinics tell their young patients about the choice of anesthetics for delivery and try to erase the gratuitous folklore that assails the ears of every first-time mother. Susan's mother is on the lookout for anxieties, spoken or unspoken. She has already disabused Susan of the notion that raising her arms will strangle the baby in the cord. Clinics usually have to debunk rumors girls exchange among themselves. The big message of clinics is that pregnancy is not a disease and you can live normally even though you're going to have a baby.

Pregnancy is not a disease, but it does depress the mother-to-be occasionally, and tire young bodies not yet finished with their own growth. "Be understanding but not indulgent," says Dr. Nix. "Backs do get to aching and an occasional forgiveness of dishwashing duty goes a long way to promote understanding."

Another important contribution parents can make at this stage is to assure that their daughter continues her edu-

cation. Finishing high school is a highly important ele-
ment in strengthening chances to live a successful, happy
life. Up until as recently as 1968, pregnant teens were
routinely put out of school the moment their condition
became apparent. If Susan wants to keep on at her old
school, she has the right, though only recently has it been
spelled out. The matter was made clear in 1972. "Every
girl in the U.S. has a right to and a need for the education
that will help her prepare herself for a career, for family
life and for citizenship," said the U.S. Commissioner of
Education. "To be married or pregnant is not sufficient
cause to deprive her of an education and the opportunity
to become a contributing member of society."

The commissioner went on to include the young
fathers in this dictum. "Young fathers also require assistance to enable them to meet the considerable responsibilities which they have assumed."

Even though the rights of girls like Susan are thus
spelled out, there are still school principals and teachers
who want to get youngsters who are obviously pregnant
out of sight. They may suggest adult night school, which
is certainly a possibility if the teen mother-to-be prefers.
But she may remain in her familiar classroom if that is
what she wants, and it is important for her to know this.
The local superintendent of schools will discuss the best
arrangement with interested parents.

States interpret "sufficient opportunity for education" differently and some assign tutors from the Department of Education for the homebound, which may include teens like Susan. Other states provide special classes
for pregnant school girls through 600 affiliates of the National Alliance Concerned with School-Age Parents. The
Tracey Education Center in Cerritos, California, is one
such center which also works closely with the community.
Here the curriculum is extended to include many of the

same things offered at a maternal or child health clinic. It has been particularly successful with young school drop-outs, who are attracted by the small classes and individ-ualized study. Three years after it opened, 74 percent of the girls who transferred to the Center's teen-mother program were either still in school or had graduated from high school. Nationally, 80 percent of teen mothers drop out, an alarming figure indeed, although careful research indicates that many would have dropped out anyway since they include a vulnerable segment of schoolagers.

Learning in the special classes conducted at the adolescent maternity clinics can be a positive experience to which teen mothers-to-be can relate. Parenting, house care, cooking, and sewing are all subjects suddenly deeply interesting to them. Studying these things also helps to make the adolescent understand that the baby is a reality. In a good clinic, the fact of the baby's existence will be affirmed to the young girls perhaps for the first time. Studies show that many young mothers-to-be have doubts they can love the baby. To their mind, they are not having a baby, they are simply pregnant. Sewing clothes for the small expected human helps make it clearer, as it has for generations, that the teen is actually going to become a mother.

The clinics are supportive in another important way: they bring together adolescents with the same prob-lem. For the first time, some of these young girls will realize they are not alone. They will experience the spe-cial attention that may have been sadly lacking in their lives and may even discover from their predicament the strength to give them a different perception of their individuality.

It's tough to make decisions while you're pregnant, especially when all the alternatives are difficult, but all young girls waiting at their parents' home to have the baby must ultimately decide how the infant will be cared for. This waiting period is the time for the mother-to-be to plan ahead. She could, of course, stay home and devote full time to raising the baby. Or, if she has a working mother, as Susan and so many others now do, the two of them and her father could perhaps arrange different shifts so that someone would always be at home. But if she isn't prepared for this kind of life—and few teenagers are—she can try to arrange foster care for the baby. She could also apply to a group residence, a new plan just getting under-way in which teen mothers live communally and can leave their babies in the care of child-care counselors while they go out to school or to work. Unfortunately, there are at present few of these in the country, though a shining example among the 4 or 5 in New York City is the Louise Wise Services, a residence supported by private philanthropy and the city's Human Resource allowances. Located in a stately old brownstone full of cheer and friendliness, this is more than a baby-sitting facility. Child-rearing skills are enhanced during the young mother's stay which may extend up to 2 years under special cir-cumstances. A staff consisting of psychiatrist, psycholo-gist, and pediatrician contributes to needs of these new mothers (fathers may visit) and their babies. Volunteers play an active part in making this residence work.

    The need for additional residential programs for single adolescent mothers inspired a "Wingspread" con-ference on this problem in 1978, under the sponsorship of the Johnson Foundation with the cooperation of the Child Welfare League of America and the Florence Crit-tenton Services of Charlotte, N.C. About 460 mothers and their infants are now receiving help at Florence Crit-tenton Centers throughout the United States.

The homes are building continuous research into their programs to examine the benefits of the comprehensive services they offer. The Wingspread conference made it clear there is a need for additional residential parent training facilities. Residential agencies not only instruct teenage mothers on the best care for their babies, some of whom are born prematurely or with birth defects, but monitor the growth and development of the infants. An average stay of six months in such a residence is necessary while an extensive network of other agencies is marshalled to help the mother face the difficult physical, psychological, and social task of rearing a baby alone.

A young mother wishing financial support for herself or care for her baby must get in touch with a state or locally administered public welfare or social services agency, often listed in the phone book under Human Resources division. Her parents may or may not be responsible for her, depending on the public welfare regulations in the state in which she lives. If she is 15 or under, they probably are; if she is 18 or over, they are probably not. Foster care and welfare allowances are both a possibility, but each state sets its own rules. A caseworker reviewing the situation will apply pertinent regulations. No appointments are made for welfare applicants and long lines may make applying an impersonal process in larger cities.

Aid to Families with Dependent Children (AFDC), the largest specific welfare program, funded about 60 percent by federal funds and balanced by state funds, varies its regulations from state to state. In no state does the applicant receive more than 90 percent of established need in cash, which averages between $107 and $160 a month for mother and baby. She is also eligible for other benefits such as Medicaid for prenatal care and delivery, payments for later illnesses of her and her baby, food stamps, and an occasional rent subsidy. If her baby is of low weight, a frequent problem in infants born to teenage mothers, she may get an additional government allotment. If the mother is living in a household already receiving AFDC, the baby is allowed only the percentage allotted to an additional family member.

If the young mother is unwilling or unable to remain with her family, she can establish herself as "emancipated" if she has reached the age of 18. Each region establishes the circumstances under which she will get a standard allotment as head of a household—seldom more than $320 monthly, at best.

She may also apply for foster care for the infant and herself to supplement whatever she can afford to pay on her own. This is to be a temporary arrangement paid by welfare according to regional scale. The mother's plans to take care of the baby can frequently falter and often the baby flounders from foster home to home, a poor candidate ultimately for adoption.

New federal rulings insist that efforts be made to establish paternity and obtain support from the putative father. A young girl on AFDC must cooperate with these efforts unless they show cause for "serious and identifiable emotional harm."

The government now thinks that assisting young mothers to stay in school is a good investment. One third of the youngest mothers who receive AFDC did not complete high school—nearly 2½ times the proportion of those who do manage to complete high school. A program in your area aimed at helping young mothers stay in school or to receive appropriate vocational training may provide day care, transportation, and an allowance according to need if the locality makes the federally supported educational option available. See your local welfare department for further information.

Day care is an essential service if young mothers are going to benefit from these programs to better themselves educationally and fit into a job market. In many communities resources for infants and young children are lacking. High cost for groups with good standards blocks the way for many. Expenditures for these services have too often been regarded as "baby-sitting" by congressional appropriations committees. Teenagers are more likely to be forced onto welfare rolls than those who defer childbearing. Half the over $9 billion the U.S. government is spending on AFDC goes to households with mothers who have given birth in their teens. Contrary to popular opinion, welfare programs do not provide an incentive to early childbearing; the fact that a majority of young girls do not want to become mothers while they are in their teens has been reconfirmed by Drs. Melvin Zelnik and John Kantner in 1976 research at Johns Hopkins.

The expense of a baby with no responsible father seems to fall hardest on the middle-class family that opts to include the infant in its own circle. The cost of having a baby was set in a congressional report by Joseph Califano, Secretary of HEW, at $1,600, including all prenatal, delivery, and postpartum services.

During the first year of life a baby will cost $1,835 these days, inflation's impact on the 1958 cost of $579. This estimate is offered by research planners on the Community Council of Greater New York and is based on a modest living level. The price of raising a baby born between 1978 and 1998, from birth to 18, has been projected at $84,000—allowing for inflation—and that is without a college education. It can be a serious dislocation of family funds to take care of a mother and child until they are self-supporting. The alternative is a serious cost to the taxpayer.

However families struggle to work it out, having a pregnant daughter at home is not easy. Nine months is a long time. If you are 15, it is a large proportion of your lifetime. Adolescent pregnancy can create a psychologically wearing situation and too often involves a downward spiral of the self-image of the teen mother-to-be. She longs for the companionship of her contemporaries, but the things that consume their interest no longer are part of her world. A pregnant teen cannot talk about her prom dress and probably not about the last basketball game. At home, the tolerant parents may be unwittingly difficult and, if there is a grandmother about, the teen may have lost face with her.

Wise parents will do all they can to ensure that their daughter gets something to think about besides her clumsy appearance and her minor physical discomforts during these long months. Learning to cook can be a good idea, and typing lessons or computer training even better, for they will start her on the way to independence in the world which she will ultimately re-enter as a wage earner. Or get her interested in sewing, especially in making clothes for herself. There's a big psychological lift in looking attractive. In some cities, older women have created a program as part of the Big Sister organization (listed in the phone book) which could encourage such activities. California works especially closely with the Big Sisters.

Parents locked into accepting a grandchild for which they are ill-prepared often berate themselves with the old self-reproach, "Where did I fail my daughter?" Try to remember that it probably wasn't you but a combination of factors which led to your daughter's difficulty, and in any case, you now have a second chance to reassess your relationship. Avoid any signs of reproach in the inevitable moments of irritation. Don't remind her, in moments of stress, that the situation is all of her own making. Never say, "Look what you've done to us."

But if you do get angry, remember that this is natural. Perhaps you are being asked to do things that you would really prefer not to do. At the very best, your feelings about this pregnancy are apt to be ambivalent. This is understandable and normal.

Continued feelings of depression and worry as your daughter's pregnancy progresses may indicate a need to turn for help to Family Service Society, the Catholic Charities Organization, or a trusted physician or clergyman. They are accustomed to offering counsel at such trying times as these.

9

Working for Community Change

Up until now, we have focused on strategies for coping with teenagers within the home.

But if you are truly committed to combatting the problem of too-early pregnancy, there is a larger area in which parents can participate—that of the surrounding community.

Dr. Erik Erikson, the eminent Harvard psychoanalyst, has mapped the stages of the human life cycle and points out that in middle age—or what he refers to as the seventh stage of adult development—parents may be concerned not only with their own family but with the state of society as a whole, both now and in future generations. What better way to work for the general good than in the area of adolescent sexuality—an area in which every community needs enlightened opinion makers and improved resources.

How can concerned parents make their voices heard?

Most importantly, through promoting sex education. This is an issue which badly needs the support of intelligent, thinking adults. It is vital to see that children learn to make responsible sex decisions and that the battle be joined in by the schools.

There is enormous work to be done. Only six states and the District of Columbia today require sex education programs of any kind. Even in these seven areas, 60 percent of the schools exclude the topic of birth control. The Alan Guttmacher Institute reports that in comprehensive programs for *pregnant* teenagers, 76 percent do not include birth control instruction.

The subject is controversial. Many parents are uneasy about putting sex instruction before pubescent children. But it seems clear that we must choose between the current upsurge of adolescent pregnancy and plain-spoken information before the fact. Said John D. Rockefeller III in a 1978 report to the Congressional House Committee on Population, a few months before his death in the fall of 1978: "The truth is that we know next to nothing about the state of sexual learning in our society except that all too many adults—parents and teachers— still consider the subject as too controversial. I should make it clear that I speak of sexual learning. I mean not just the biology and mechanics of sex, but the moral values and responsibilities, the sense of concern and caring for others as well as one's self, that should permeate this most natural and important aspect of human life."

Rockefeller was a pragmatist. His interest for the

new generation was centered upon translating concern into action.

"When human beings pass the age of puberty," he said, "they are going to engage in sex sooner or later, and nothing is going to stop them. I believe that most teenagers want to be responsible about sex. To do so, they must have an opportunity to learn about the responsibilities involved and they must be able to control their own fertility. . . ."

For parents who agree about the importance of sex education, a big job remains to be done. In Michigan, birth control could not even be discussed in any school until a 10-year battle was won in the legislature late in 1977. The long debate, centered on repealing the legislation outlawing mention of family planning, brought out the general issue of sex education. Barbara-Rose Collins, a black member of the Michigan house and an outspoken supporter of freedom of birth control information, declared during the proceedings:

> . . . the unwed mother situation is a curse. The reason it's a curse is that black girls who don't get an abortion will keep their babies — they won't be adopted. It just isn't in the black family tradition to do that. But there you are. You don't have a job. You've never had a job or work experience. You don't know how to raise a child; you haven't raised yourself yet. So you turn to welfare. It doesn't take much to figure welfare is a form of slavery because the government . . . can tell you where you can live, what you wear . . . what kind of food you eat. I've seen it happen, and my concern centers on the girl children who are forced to face all this after being denied basic, simple information.

Although the figures for black teenage pregnancy exceed those for white, too-early motherhood is a problem for all. Reports from the Michigan state senators' own neighborhoods proved that parents in all districts were struggling with the same difficulty. In Grand Rapids, State Senator John Otterbacker seemed to express the case for pragmatic agreement with passage of the 1977 Michigan bill allowing birth control information when he said, ". . . moral issue or not, many teenagers do not have accurate sexual facts and as a result end up with unwanted pregnancies, abortions, suicides, divorces."

Arizona faced different problems from Michigan. Although a bill incorporating sex education in Arizona was passed in 1977, implementation has depended on individual teachers and school principals, and parents in this state can withhold permission for their children to attend such classes. This arrangement was a compromise coming out of a well-organized fight by the Movement to Restore Decency in Education that, for 8 years, defeated each bill introduced in the legislature to allow sex education in schools. On the opposite side of the controversy was the Arizona Medical Association, which was alarmed by the upward surge of pregnancies among girls 12 to 14 years old. Arizona, then as now, led the nation in gonorrhea cases and the doctors were convinced that good health education was sorely needed.

It is important to realize that vocal parents opposed to sex education for their children have incalculable effects on what is offered all other children as well. "The administrators are afraid of the parents' static," says Margaret Duncan, director of the Pima County Division of Arizona Health Education. Her division has had its share of trouble convincing the public of the need to start sex education at junior high level, even though studies show that junior-high-school girls in Pima are becoming pregnant earlier and earlier.

Changes in local policy come slowly. Take the case of Fairfax County in Northern Virginia, where 23 high schools, comprising 40,000 students, use a standard curriculum provided by the Board of Education. In 1969 there was an effort in this suburban neighborhood to hold hearings on developing a teaching program on sex education. The Movement to Restore Decency in Education successfully opposed such open discussion. As time passed, however, pressure was brought to bear to reconsider proposing a sex education curriculum. A public hearing was called for the presentation of the plan outlined by the superintendent of schools. Two evening meetings were scheduled for mid-November 1976.

Each meeting was attended by over 100 people, with more than 50 listed to speak. Each speaker was given 5 minutes to present his or her viewpoint and invited to leave documents further developing that opinion. The discussion revealed opposing positions and it continued well into the night. Many became thoughtful when Louise Winfield, a citizen concerned that all students should have an opportunity for comprehensive sex education, said in part:

We will be safer on the roads and highways because last year Fairfax County provided driver education for some nine thousand students. . . . I am not suggesting that learning to handle a car and to know and follow the rules of the road is comparable to learning to understand one's sexual nature and acquiring sexual attitudes and practices which will promote personal fulfillment and social well-being. I am reminding us that there was a time when driving instruction was not a part of a school curriculum because automobiles were not an essential part of school communities. When transportation patterns changed, the school program changed.

A new generation must deal with its fertility in new and responsible ways. We can feel more secure about the future, and our young people can feel happier about their emerging manhood and womanhood, when sex education classes begin. We must not hesitate to give this county's children the help they want to better understand themselves, and the knowledge and incentive they need to be mindful of their own, and of the common good as they make their choices in the deeply human and highly spiritual dimension of life called Sex.

The Board of Education was left to make the decision on how to construct the curriculum based on controversial feelings expressed on all sides. It revised the curriculum to eliminate certain filmstrips, explicit photos or diagrams, and certain textbooks. Moreover, the students would need to have parental permission to attend this compromise sex education course offered within regular school hours. Parents were invited to join their children in the classroom. No free or spontaneous discussion was permitted. Questions by students were submitted in writing prior to class. Four subjects were listed as prohibited: homosexuality, contraception, masturbation, and abortion. However, frank discussion on intercourse, VD, and concern about values and attitudes were encouraged.

One year later, an evaluation in the form of a student questionnaire seems to conclude, according to an administration spokesman, that the students believe the sex education course is essentially worthless. The students indicated that they wished to move beyond a study of the reproductive system to information on how they can prevent pregnancy or get contraceptive help. Based on this first year's experience, a report will be given to the public with the hope of developing next steps.

Fairfax was, however, the scene of a small triumph when Lauren Boyd and Gina Gambino, students at Hayfield High School, gathered opinions about sex attitudes among their classmates.

Their data collected, Lauren wrote an article about the results for the school paper, but school officials, backed by the school board, refused to allow it to be printed. Ably supported by the Law Center of the Student Press in Washington, D.C., the two students charged that their First Amendment rights had been violated and the Federal District Court agreed. The article ran.

The initial censored article revealed that a high percentage of sexually active Hayfield High School students were not acquainted with basic birth control facts and used no contraception.

Said the article, in part: "The sex education proposed by Fairfax County does not in any way contribute to the students' knowledge of birth control methods. . . . Birth control information . . . will not lead to 'immorality' and 'promiscuity' among students . . . There are enough people at Hayfield whose values have already been set . . . and their moral standards will not be altered by teaching birth control in school."

School officials had defended banning the article on the grounds that it offered birth control advice, information not given out in class, and they would not permit a student newspaper to provide information not permitted in classroom teaching.

The fact that the two students were willing to fight

for their rights, and won, may make it easier for others. The National Organization of Non-Parents subsequently promoted a nationwide contest for the best article by a student on sex education.

Only ten miles from Hayfield the situation is very different. Here in the George Mason Junior-Senior High School in Falls Church, Virginia, for the last 7 years a sex information program has been attracting nationwide attention. Mary Lee Tatum, its articulate, energetic director, feels strongly about how human sexuality should be presented in high schools.

"We care very much that sexuality be treated as a serious subject," says Tatum, "not only for facts but for feelings. We put in a course on it, right along with the three R's. What our culture has bought is 'sex is sin but isn't it fun.' At the core, this is very titillating and, for adolescents, it represents a very confusing message."

The public schools in Falls Church have an elective sex education program beginning in the sixth grade where a basic reproductive anatomy course touching on physical and emotional maturing and social attitudes within the peer group is taught. Eighth-graders can sign up for several sex-related discussion groups during the year. The focus in these seminars is on what the students want to know, and this turns out mostly to be about relationships, attitudes, and basic sex matters.

Ninth-graders get a year-long class called Life Science, which includes anatomy, physiology, psychology, and sociology all rolled into one, with heavy emphasis on family life and human sexuality. Seniors can take an optional 9-week senior seminar on human sexuality.

Parents should take note that this comprehensive program grew from a community-school committee formed to take up the matter of sex education. Public hearings were held and parents invited to discuss what they thought would be relevant to students' needs in this course.

There was inevitable controversy. The Falls Church group fielded doubts on the advisability of teaching facts on homosexuality, masturbation, and contraception by emphasizing that the courses offered a serious forum for the discussion of these matters, in contrast to the prevailing sly wink and off-color joke. Leaders of the group told parents that it was useless to think they could protect their children from learning about the issues they questioned when they were confronted daily with a media blitz on these very subjects. Tatum and her group explained that their mission was to help students sort out the information from the misinformation.

When one of the early senior seminars closed, a young male participant left behind this endorsement:

"I've heard my friends in this class discussing sex seriously for the first time. Before it's always been a jab in the ribs, a dirty joke, and lots of dishonest talk. You know, the discussion of sex will never be that way for me again."

Regrettably, many schools continue to offer students courses which fail to give them a well-rounded perception of human sexuality. Often hygiene courses masquerade as sex education. A good early course about sex should include the broad spectrum of psychology, physiology, anatomy, and sociology, together with practical information on how to avoid pregnancy and where to go to get contraceptive help.

The PTA should represent a true majority and it is important to speak out to make your voice heard. Tatum once convened a meeting at which only twelve persons showed up, all of whom represented positive support. They came because they were afraid dissenters might try to vote out sex education if they stayed home. The Board of Education is quick to look at sex education as a frill if the budget gets tight and there is no evidence of parental enthusiasm.

Evaluation of parents' support of the Falls Church program was undertaken by the George Mason High School in the program's third year of operation. Dr. Susan Philliber, representing the Columbia University College of Physicians and Surgeons Center for Population and Family Health, introduced and analyzed a questionnaire sent to all parents of the senior high school. Almost half responded to the query. Of these, 84 percent answered affirmatively to the question, "Would you recommend to other parents that your son or daughter take the sex-education course offered in the high school?"

Fifty-six percent of these same parents reported that they had had a significant sex-related discussion with their sons and daughters in the last two months. There appears to be a new freedom derived from open discussion at school.

What it comes down to is that home and school must work together.

Louise Winfield, students at Hayfield High, and progressive parents in the Fairfax community made their voices heard. What are some other strategies for fostering sex education on the local level?

The Syracuse, New York, project undertaken by the Institute for Family Research and Education recommends conducting an opinion poll on community attitudes toward sex education to use as a baseline when arguing for needed change. An hour-long TV show, "Sex, Can It Teach Itself?" is also available from the Institute free of charge for showing at local church and civic meetings (see Resource Guide).

National Family Sex Education Week offers another springboard for action in enlisting community support for sex education. Endorsed by Planned Parenthood, the PTA, churches, and professional and political leaders, this is an annual October event in many areas. Interested parents should get in touch with their local educational, religious, and youth-serving groups for further information. The week is dedicated to the philosophy that ignorance, not knowledge, stimulates inappropriate sexual behavior.

Concerned parents can also look to their local libraries for support. Libraries are usually excellent partners for those backing sex education, although some shelves still contain antiquated sex education books which are misleading, if not harmful. "The real purpose of these books is not sex education but sex prevention," says Patty Campbell, a Young Adult Librarian, in a 1978 issue of the American Library Association (ALA) publication, *Top of the News,* devoted to sex and youth.

In this time of transition for libraries, the ALA has shown aggressive leadership by adopting in January 1978 a policy statement submitted by Mary K. Chelton, Professor of the Graduate School of Library Science of Rutgers University. It essentially urges "all librarians and library educators to examine existing policies and practices, and to assume a leadership role in seeing that information is available for children and adolescents, their parents, and youth-serving professionals at the state and local level, to assure that comprehensive sex-related education materials, programs, referral and health services for youth are available and publicized."

Dr. Chelton stresses the need for parent education in the area of adolescent sexuality. She says, "Too often librarians are inclined to blame parents without providing useful tools to understand their sons' and daughters' needs. The number of adolescents who might be helped by helping their parents, the primary sex educators, is inestimable."

Some school or community librarians are inhibited by fears of irate parents who are responsible for the increased incidence of book banning. (This censorship reached a peak in the 1978 school year, according to the ALA Office for Intellectual Freedom.) It is critical that concerned parents organize to bolster leaders in school or community libraries working toward the expressed library goal of free access to all aspects of sex education.

Parents who work with librarians can often help affirm their joint convictions by sorting out sex education volumes containing accurate information and meeting agreed-upon criteria. Out of such cooperation can come good dialogues about the value of books like the controversial *Forever* by Judy Blume, a novel for young people which has shocked some parents but which others think provides insight into the sexual behavior of high school students today.

Forever was the center of such a dialogue among mothers of teenagers who had read it in the town of Bath, Ohio, chronicled by Joyce Maynard for *The New York Times Sunday Magazine* of December 3, 1978. One alarmed mother saw the book as one more sign of the declining moral standards all around her. Another bemoaned the author's failure to grasp "the beautiful opportunity" to punish her characters or at least evoke feelings of guilt. To this a thoughtful mother responded. "I am not sure I would want to burden my daughter with a sense of guilt." She herself had suffered too much from her own misunderstanding of her youthful sexual feelings.

Finally a mother remarked, "You can be a nice girl and have a love affair. You would be surprised at the caliber of girls I see at the Planned Parenthood clinic where I volunteer." This encouraged another mother to add, "Though I can't condone *Forever,* I am glad my daughter read it. It is like birth control; I am not going to give it to her, but if she has an affair, I would certainly rather have her use it. I hope she will wait until she is married, like I did."

Forever was certainly a groundbreaker and stimulated an odd sort of black market upon its appearance, since some parents, like those in Bath, were fearful that reading about early sex encounters would sanction a like pattern for their daughters, and forbade them to read the book. As a result, teens bootlegged copies when they found them hard to come by, renting chapters to exchange at bus stops. One professional in the sex education field said, "When 500 copies of a book are stolen, it is a good indication that more copies should be bought."

Although many of us worry about what our children read, there is probably no greater influence on young people today than television. Malcolm Oettinger, co-author of *The Reluctant Regulators,* a study of broadcast regulations as they affect the viewers, says that the effects of TV are of real concern to parents. Some believe that TV condones immoral behavior, makes sexual adventures seem not only acceptable but socially *de rigueur,* and keeps their children in an excited state through constant suggestiveness. TV executives, responding to angry citizen groups decrying "sex on the airwaves," point out that TV does not portray the unvarnished sexuality of X-rated or R-rated motion pictures—that nudity and intercourse are not shown on the screen. But because of the intimate and accessible nature of TV, its omnipresence in the home, it is generally regarded as a greater threat to a young person's attitudes than porno films or salacious novels. After all, youngers must seek out the latter with a tingly sense of harvesting forbidden fruit, while TV is regarded by them as the arbiter of social norms.

How can parents of this TV generation help determine that their children get the kind of information that leads to healthy sexuality?

Perhaps the most useful approach is to watch television with your children and discuss the moral implications of programs with "adult themes." If a parent feels strongly that the airwaves are supercharged with sex, he or she has several stronger alternatives available. There are citizen groups that protest officially to the Federal Communications Commission, to TV advertisers, and to networks. Some of these groups, however, seem to have a fundamentalist, vigilante attitude which can be counterproductive. Because of the First Amendment considerations that forbid government censorship, the FCC can act only in cases of blatant obscenity—which are rare on TV. However, groups have had success in writing major corporations asking them not to advertise on suggestive programs. And the defensive comments from network executives show that they, too, have some sensitivity to parents' complaints—particularly if they run a risk of reduced revenues. Letters of complaint to a network should include a copy to the viewer's local network affiliate. These stations are charged with serving their local communities—and a rash of complaints may make local programmers decide not to run network programs that many viewers consider offensive.

Religious institutions are another resource to which parents concerned with strengthening moral responsibility for reproductive behavior can turn. Adolescent sexuality has recently been a concern of the National Council of the Churches of Christ in the USA, the National Conference of Catholic Bishops, and the Synagogue Council of America. In a joint statement, these councils announced a determination to face adolescent sex as an interfaith cooperative effort. Religious leaders are aware of the new social conditions which affect the lives of the young.

Some churches and synagogues have held weekend conferences on human sexuality for youth and their parents. The United Methodist church offers state or regional conferences which include choice of speakers, films, and pamphlets. Groups working within this church have found a sexual-attitude inventory of initial attitudes an excellent place to begin, and the results have surprised nearly everybody. The young, it seems, have much the same basic attitudes as their parents, and are groping for more than rules. Interestingly, many denominations seem to have an open mind about normal sexuality in or out of marriage, confining themselves largely to whether the individuals involved are treating each other with concern.

Fathers please note:

In all these avenues to changing public opinion, the need for men's voices is especially great. While general volunteerism has increased 20 percent recently, few men are represented in the figures. Though latest Bureau of Labor statistics prove more adults are stepping forward to

lend a hand (many after eight hours on a paying job),
there are never enough men. And the volunteering
should be a continuing commitment, not one that fades in
and out of adolescent lives.

With all this talk about what parents can do in the home
and community, the importance of fighting to preserve
the constitutional rights of adolescents must not be
overlooked. Few minors have been advised of the
confirmation of these rights, which include the right to
privacy. In recent United States Supreme Court decisions
it has been determined that *minors have a constitutional
right to receive sex-related health services without
parental consent.* The court has ruled that minors are not
second-class citizens and they, like adults, have funda-
mental constitutional rights. It clearly holds that a blanket
requirement of parental consent for an abortion violates
the rights of the minor involved. Following the logic of
this case, it appears that prohibiting any sex-related
medical care, including contraception, is probably
unconstitutional.

   Some states have had laws limiting minors' access
to contraceptives. A law existed in New York State which
prohibited the sale or distribution of nonprescription birth-
control articles to minors under 16. A case was brought
challenging the constitutionality of this law. The U.S.
Supreme Court held that a state may not impose prohibi-
tion on the distribution of nonprescription contraceptives
to minors under 16 and that the law was an unconstitutional burden on minors' right to privacy. This decision,
like all U.S. Supreme Court decisions, is binding in all
states.

   Parents without special training in legal or political
matters may hesitate to involve themselves in the seem-

ingly complex issues of contraception for minors. But the only way to make *real* the objective of responsible sexual behavior is to see that those who need help in becoming as responsible as we wish them to be have access to that help. Parents who find doctors reluctant to provide birth control information to minors should know that Harriet F. Pilpel, the leading authority on laws regarding contraception and minors, has often been quoted as saying, "There is no reported case where a doctor has been convicted or held civilly liable for damages for furnishing contraceptive services to minors without parental consent."

No state expressly prohibits in all cases the provision of contraceptives to minors, though some still require parental consent under some limited circumstances.

Many parents who are involved as volunteers or policy-makers of appropriate voluntary agencies may alert their groups to become acquainted with the opportunities for local development of resources which the new Office of Adolescent Pregnancy programs will administer. When final regulations are complete and funds are appropriated by Congress HEW will begin to award grants to public or private agencies to implement an act passed in late 1978, the Adolescent Health Services and Pregnancy Prevention and Care Act, authorizing $200 million over a three-year period.

The proposed regulations state two major purposes for granting funds: "(1) assist in preventing unwanted pregnancies among adolescents and (2) assist pregnant adolescents and adolescent parents to obtain needed medical, social, educational, and other services that will help them to become productive independent contributors to family and community life."

The key to the plan is the requirement that any

applicant provide a network of "core services" such as pregnancy diagnosis, maternity counseling, family planning and educational services, and adoption counseling. Assurance is also required that pregnant adolescents will be informed of all options regarding their pregnancy.

It has been strongly suggested in the resolution of the final regulations that an adolescent not be denied pregnancy-related information and services on a basis of inability to pay fees or unwillingness to consult parents. Fears were expressed that ambiguities in the legislative language might lead only to the provision of supportive services to pregnant girls and young parents. This would not fulfill the central purpose of the prevention of adolescent pregnancy. As citizens prepare to meet the needs in their communities, it is important clearly to state the requirements for application in order to free the participating agencies to administer effectively the individual projects for which they seek support.

Dr. Irving Kushner, Deputy Assistant Secretary for Population Affairs in DHEW, says that, "coordination of services and programs to develop linkages with related agencies is an essential part of favorable consideration in awarding grants to communities."

Indicative of Congressional interest not only in pregnancy-related services but also in research, were the questions asked at the spring 1979 appropriation hearings establishing the budget for the next fiscal year. The Committee members queried what was being done in light of the high incidence of adolescent pregnancy. The Department of Health, Education and Welfare, National Institutes of Health, responded that they were currently encouraging grants to investigate various avenues of research on such questions as how much teens are influenced by the perceived risk of pregnancy; what the attitudes of the male partner are; and how much these attitudes influence sexual and contraceptual behavior.

We really do not know yet but must continue to seek answers.

As parents work either to provide or coordinate services to pregnant adolescents, to vindicate adolescents' rights to access to contraceptives, to work for sex education, or to monitor TV or other activities, they must recognize that there is no single solution to this complicated psychosocial problem. We don't fully understand how to combat the current sweeping forces that are responsible for the wave of pregnancies even in the youngest of our adolescents. We know so much more about consequences than we do causes. For this reason, we cannot expect too much too soon.

There is one thing, however, that we do know. A good mother-daughter relationship often goes hand in hand with more effective contraceptive practice. Communication between parent and child about sex may actually forestall or postpone the child's sexual activity, according to research reported by Greer Litton Fox in *Children Today* in June 1979 (U.S. Department of HEW).

It would be satisfying, says Dr. Fox, to be able to make a series of recommendations, but these would have to be based as much on what we do not know as what we do.

Nevertheless, she asserts one cardinal principle: "Ways of involving the parent or parents of teens must be developed, implemented and evaluated as a core component of all relevant programs, whether the specific program is in primary prevention or sex education, in contraceptive service provision or in pregnancy and postpartum assistance."

10

Peer Counseling: Why and How

"If you think IUD is a note to someone you owe money to and vacuum aspiration is GE's newest model electric broom, you need a visit to Room 122," says a poster that advertises a sex information center in 11 high schools in New York City's pilot peer counseling project.

What is peer counseling?

It's teens talking to teens about life and sex and the problems of growing up. It's parents and professionals reaching those vulnerable young people who are initiating sex activity at an increasingly early age. It's a natural way to turn peer identification into a positive force. This project seems so promising to the National Institute of Child Health and Human Development, that it is supporting eleven different programs nationally to explore various approaches to peer counseling.

Peer counselors have heard it all firsthand, from expert trainers with no holds barred, and they have been trained to listen. These young people know more about the current sexual scene and what is actually happening than those who have not directly experienced these conflicts. They absorb it daily in their role as trusted confidant and referral advisor. It would be difficult to know what their real influence has been, but many in the know are now saying that they have a significant effect on reducing the number of teenage pregnancies.

"By far the most popular innovative service mentioned by twenty national youth service organizations I have spoken with is peer counseling," says William Ryerson, director of Youth and Student Services of the Population Institute, a nationwide nonprofit organization.

The peer group is a natural way station between childhood dependency on the parent and the intense, almost exclusive allegiance to contemporaries. Talking with counselors of the same age, who use the same words and are part of the same social-sexual pressure cooker, offers adolescents a sense of belonging which is a basic human need and vital to them. However deeply hidden, conflict is involved in casting off parental authority, and peer counselors fill this gap, transmitting to bewildered, anxious teens accurate information about the things that worry them.

There's nothing fundamentally new about adolescents getting together to talk about sex; teenagers have been pooling such information for decades. But a lot of erroneous facts have traditionally been handed along in this time-honored fashion. Plenty of adolescents have douched with Coke or stood up during intercourse because their contemporaries told them they wouldn't get pregnant that way. Peer counseling gives teens the *real* answers to their questions.

Peer counseling is more than the old bull session. It wears an enlightened new face, and is now a rap situation in which truth and knowledge are exchanged instead of ignorance shared. The word "rap," by the way, is in the dictionary today. Webster defines it as talking freely and frankly with people with similar interests and problems. If everybody feels at ease and comfortable with one another, as well as secure in the knowledge that what is said will not be repeated, things get ironed out. Eighty percent of adolescents consulting Planned Parenthood counselors were referred by their satisfied friends.

Peer counseling groups are springing up all over the country and each uses a slightly different approach, depending on the community and the people involved. In Washington, D.C., peer counseling in sex education is funded by a grant from the Cafritz Foundation to Planned Parenthood of Metropolitan Washington. The money has been used to set up three rap rooms in three area high schools and a Sex Information Center in a fourth. The counselors are trained for fifteen weeks and then act as what PPMW calls translators, interpreting information gleaned from their training course on birth control, human sexuality, pregnancy, venereal disease, and anything else that worries their contemporaries. Settings that make teens feel at home include bright paint, rugs, and throw pillows. Free literature and a small library are provided. On opening day at the first of these centers, the entire school was invited to a film on sexuality.

At the Sex Information Center in Washington (in operation for an experimental period), the counselors advertise their own services on bulletin boards with bright, intriguing posters. They have held a film fair covering birth control, VD, pregnancy, and dating relationships. Operating expenses are minimal. Most decorations and printing costs are contributed by the students themselves and their parents, an invaluable factor in making the students feel the service is truly their own.

Becoming a peer counselor is a serious business. This new movement has tried to weed out the inevitable areas of ignorance and possible bias of the students who volunteer for training. Candidates get highly sophisticated preparation from sex educators, tough drilling in sex facts, broad exposure to both right- and left-wing schools of thought about sex. In some cities, they listen to representatives from Right to Life and Gay Lib. Great emphasis is put on learning to conceal both shock and amusement at what they hear from the students reaching out for help. By the time they are ready for the final exam, they are completely unruffled by such questions as "How many times can I have intercourse without getting pregnant?" or "Is it really true I'll get pimples if I masturbate?"

In the Washington training program, peer counselors emerge with an unusually broad knowledge of male and female anatomy and the medical terms to replace those in common street use. They have increased responsibility and listening skills and know the value of working in a group for a common cause. They are comfortable with their own sexuality and have gained confidence in making decisions, a skill fairly rare in the young. They have learned how to accept the problems of others in a nonjudgmental manner.

"To me, being a peer counselor in human sexuality means being able to reach things that matter," said one student on his final "sexam," as the kids call it. "There are many pregnancies out here that could have been prevented if the partners were alert."

"It helped me get to know people and learn their feelings as well as my own," said another.

What can you, as an interested parent, do to initiate a peer training program in your community?

An excellent reference source is *Sex Counseling by Telephone* (see Resource Guide). It is the work of the leaders of a counseling and sex education department for clients with sexual problems set up by Preterm Institute of Boston, a center for reproductive health. The text deals with what the founders learned in this program, including everything that bears on peer counseling. It outlines a structured, 6-week program designed to serve as a model for setting up training for interested young people, and explores a good deal of information on sexual mores uncovered at Preterm. Information on how to train counselors, how they can best offer help and understanding, what types of calls to expect, and what resources can be used for referral are all provided.

Preterm's manual offers a few tips learned during the setting up of their program. Among them:

1. Screen applicants for counseling carefully, weeding out those who are very conservative and those whose questionnaires reveal either a difficult history of sexual upbringing or too repressive a one that has obviously not been worked out since. Watch out for hostile or withdrawn candidates.

2. Two 3-hour sessions of training a week for 9 weeks plus an all-day session following the second meeting has been found to be a good schedule. Too-long intervals between tend to make the course fragmented.

3. An ideal group consists of 1 male and 1 female leader and 20 participants. Two leaders means that the group can be broken down into smaller groups.

4. An informal atmosphere is better than a class-room setting.

The Teen Advocacy Project under the auspices of the California Union of Primary Health Providers also has been successful with peer counselors. The counselors of this group are paid—slightly above the minimum wage— and the program is beamed toward the community. The teens work 10 hours a week, 5 of them devoted to what the group calls "outreach" work in the community. They are trained to serve as the critical link between the various community agencies, high schools, clinics, and the young people themselves. They act as referral agents, and what they learn they communicate to adults for use in inter-preting the needs and attitudes of the teen population.

The advocates, as California prefers to call them, are encouraged to start their outreach with people they already know. The program hopes to use the ever-widen-ing circle created by word of mouth to exchange informa-tion among the young. The adolescent advocates are chosen especially for motivation and creativity, and are encouraged to run things as they see best.

The California project is specifically beamed at an audience of sexually active teenagers who do not use medically prescribed means of birth control. Only 10-15 percent avail themselves of birth control advice from con-traceptive clinics, and the project feels the advocate pro-gram is most needed among the other 85 percent.

The youngsters use the "calling card" method, leaving bright yellow cards advertising their services at local community hangouts, parks and beaches, school campuses. They also make contact with high-school counselors and health and biology teachers. They work closely with the Ys, three local churches, the Red Cross, and a local Teen Post sponsored by the Advocacy Project. They look for speaking engagements at health fairs and community events and it is interesting that, to date, a high percentage of the cards left have been brought back to them by uneasy adolescents seeking real answers to their sex problems.

Another approach is that offered for a limited time in 11 of New York City's high schools, where a pilot peer counseling project has been tried out. Each of the schools set aside a rap room for a cooperative effort between students, teachers, parents, and the community that other schools might well emulate.

The key factor in New York was student involvement, for the project was organized because of student demand. It grew from the dissatisfaction of a group of students who felt that their sex education was deficient. They formed the Student Coalition for Relevant Sex Education. The young people asked the Bureau of Health and Physical Education to help them and developed, with their cooperation, a peer sex-information program funded by the Ford Foundation.

In New York City, the young people invited each high-school principal to participate and to suggest a teacher, usually in the health department, who was popular with students and might be named advisor. This teacher was then responsible for finding a rap room, publicizing the project, and recruiting students for peer counseling.

Volunteers in the program were rigorously trained by the teacher/advisor and a specialist from the Bureau of Health and Physical Education. As part of this training, the counselors visited neighborhood clinics and agencies where they might refer students coming to them. The counselors from all the high schools met together once a month to share common problems and information, and to receive further training.

A different sort of program attests to what one voice can do—in this case the voice of a determined school nurse in California.

Sure that the problems dumped daily in her lap by troubled teens were not really health problems but sex problems, this young woman took matters in her own hands. The parents had obviously been unprepared to give proper instruction and were looking to the school for help. After receiving permission from school authorities, she called a meeting of parents and, flanked by health authorities, suggested that what was needed was a school sex information center. Today this community has an active peer counseling group. Ten years ago in such a conservative community this would have been unthinkable. One reason we have been so long in making use of teen-to-teen sex rap sessions is that such matters have long been something "genteel" people did not talk about in public.

A shining example of what a peer counseling program can be, and a leader from the start, is the one at Yale University, where directors of the Yale Sexuality Program report that less than 3 percent of the women become pregnant. More than 95 percent of those having intercourse use adequate contraception. The Yale program reaches out to students in many ways. A noncredit human sexuality course is offered, combining standard lectures with student-led discussions. Tapes are made of these lectures so that other students may hear them, and sexual counseling by peers is available in the evening. A paperback, *Sex at Yale,* prepared by the students themselves, is given to every entering student, and it is so successful that hundreds of other universities have asked for copies and many have emulated the program. Subjects included are male and female anatomy, sexual intercourse and response, contraception, pregnancy testing, abortion, and VD.

The training for all peer counseling deals with both facts and attitudes. How the students themselves feel about sex is an important part of counseling and it is vital to eliminate any possible previous hangups. To this end, explicit sex films are sometimes shown so that the young people may learn that sex is different for different people. Dr. Mary Calderone, writing in a SEICUS newsletter with Michael Carrera, professor of health education at Hunter College, says she considers it vital that those who advise "get in touch with, cope with and grow with themselves as sexual beings" before dealing with anxieties of those they advise.

The late Isadore Rubin, a noted expert in the field, often pointed out that it is impossible to reach a consensus on sexual values. He noted that perhaps in no other area of human behavior was there so much diversity in attitudes, feelings and actions as there was in the area of sexuality.

Add to this the fact that sexual problems are emotionally loaded. "You don't make a decision about sex. You just do it," said one girl, and it is unfortunately often true. One of a peer counselor's most important jobs is to communicate to those who come with their problems the vital need to make up their minds in advance what they will do when opportunity arises. In this way there should be fewer crisis decisions.

Like everything else, peer counseling has its critics.

Some fault it because it provides advice *before* adolescents get into trouble. Doesn't this encourage promiscuity? Dr. Marjorie McKusick, former president of the
Association for Adolescent Medicine, says she thinks "it
occasionally does, but it is a much greater crime to ignore
teen problems until they lead to the creation of an
unwanted child."

Other critics question the ability of the young counselors. "Aren't we asking too much of the kids involved in
these programs?" demanded one participant in a consor-
tium on early childbearing and child rearing held by the
Child Welfare League of America, Inc. "You can't put the
burden of correcting society on a teen rap session."

True enough. But experts in the field who are
enthusiastic about peer programs feel that the responsibility can and must be shared through an adequate
referral system. Michael Carrera explains the special role
of peer counseling like this: "One of the real problems for
young people is that they are reaching a point in their
lives where they have tremendous needs for accurate
information and guidance, but they also want independence from adults. With this program, they can have their
information and not compromise their independence
because they can go to someone who is an equal."

Indeed, in the final analysis, the relationship may
be as important as the information handed on.

"Kids in a counseling situation become something
of a peer family, like brothers and sisters," says a practic-
ing Chicago psychoanalyst. "There doesn't have to be a
barrier between teens and adults, but there often is." Peer
counseling makes it possible to get around this difficulty.

My own belief is that peer counseling is a valuable
tool which is rightly more and more accepted. I think that

we must reach out to our children in the ways in which we can be heard, take advantage of the methods that work best. The young tend to trust each other, and especially with adequate supervision—and this is very important—peer counseling is a force that may well make a dent on too-early pregnancy.

One of the most interesting things about peer counseling is what it does for the counselors themselves.

The Child Welfare League quotes one peer counselor on her experience:

"I went into the program not trusting anyone. I felt I was cracking up. I went to peer group because of sex . . . Sex was a big hangup.

"People seemed interested in me. It made me feel good. I started getting into it. Later I began training to become one of the students working in the program.

"I've changed a lot, learned a lot. I'm contacting people. I'm not like them, but I can understand what they do—like getting pregnant. Through the peer group I've opened up. I can say what I want to say. Now I can trust people. I have more confidence."

And mark these last words:

"I can talk to my parents."

11

Innovative Programs Tailored to Teens

A 13-year-old gingerly changes a diaper. Another wipes a 2-year-old's runny nose. In the corner a 14-year-old is awkwardly holding a baby in her arms and administering a bottle.

Boys and girls, hardly more than children themselves, are taking a course in a parenting program established in many regions by the National Center of Child Advocacy. The courses operate with the help of grants from the Office of Child Development and the National Institute of Mental Health with the support of the Office of Education.

The program aims at junior- and senior-high-school students and gives them a chance to work with young children in the double-barreled hope that they can learn about human development and find out something about themselves. Field-tested in over 500 public schools, it makes it possible for adolescents to spend 2 or more hours a week in day-care centers and kindergartens. The program's developers hope that this will give the participants a better understanding of the biological and social forces shaping a growing child and the part they may play in helping these particular children. It aims not only to give them some idea of the pleasures involved in rearing a child but to pinpoint the responsibilities entailed in bringing another human being into the world.

Does it work?

Listen to what some of the youngsters say.

"Before I went in I thought I'd get married right away and have children. Now, I want to wait until I'm mature enough to be a good parent," says a boy who has worked in this course.

Raising children of your own is a monumental job under the best of circumstances and, as another participant in the course said, "it does help to make us better parents and adults. Most kids don't learn what we have until much later in life. It's like a headstart."

Adolescents in this course not only get firsthand knowledge of the demands small children make on their parents but this pseudo-parenting brings the students into contact with a wide variety of cultures ranging from Mexican-American and urban black to that of a New England lobster fisherman's family. The course comes with auxiliary films and booklets that can be ordered from Exploring Childhood (see Resource Guide).

In setting up the program, its project director, E. Dollie Wolverton, worked with 7 youth organizations ranging from the Boy Scouts (whose members earn a merit badge in this course) to the 4-H. She speaks enthusiastically of its success.

"Education is basic prevention," she says. "Adolescents who see firsthand the responsibilities of caring for young children are less apt to rush into having babies than are the uninitiated."

Parents are badly needed to support this program, says Wolverton, who has visited 240 areas where her program is operative. "Parents can affect what courses are offered, influence the school. I have seen it work."

Wolverton, like Dr. Jones, emphasizes the need for male participation: Boys need to learn to share the responsibility for bringing up children. They need to learn along with the girls that parenting, as William Raspberry, *Washington Post* columnist, says, "is hard work, not an escape from anything." Emily Moore, director of Planned Parenthood of Metropolitan Washington, says that all young people get a sense of the reality of child-rearing from these courses, giving them the basis for an "intelligent choice between having children and not having children." Wolverton never says to the students of her course, "*When* you have children . . ." She says instead, with a sense of implied choice, "*If* you have children . . ."

The Red Cross is another organization which has come up with fresh ammunition in the battle to dissuade youngsters from unthinking acceptance of premature parenthood. Their Project Girl, which offers courses in extended baby and child care in coordination with other organizations like the Campfire Girls and the Girls Club of America, is getting far more emphasis.

In line with the belief that local chapters can best understand their own needs, the National Red Cross has left the implementation of Project Girl up to each community. In Delaware, groups of teens are now exploring attitudes and feelings about parenthood in rap sessions— and incidentally sharing information. In Indiana, one Red

Cross chapter is extending the Big Sisters program to serve troubled adolescents. In Kingsport, Tennessee, the chapter is joining forces with the Girls Club to expand sexual knowledge. Clara Barton would most certainly have approved.

Using a new setup called Rock Project, a third group, the Population Institute, is fighting fire with fire in its attempt to expand opportunities for adolescents to get sex education and counseling. Disturbed by the influence of hard rock and R-rated movies, the Institute is working hard to counterbalance confusing messages pouring out of the media. Rock Project offers public-service spots taped by such stars as Alice Cooper and Loretta Lynn at no cost to any radio station wishing to air them. Each 30-60-second spot is a hard-hitting message about the drawbacks of too-early childbearing and pregnancy.

If star athletes and rock singers can sell beer and cigarettes, possibly they can sell the idea of birth control. Says running back Lawrence McCutcheon of the Los Angeles Rams on the subject of being a parent, "I think I'm probably still a little wild, so I just have to settle down a little more." Says basketball great Kareem Abdul-Jabbar, "If you are going to enjoy the pleasures of sex, you have to be willing to deal with the results."

The spots are lifted from personal interviews so that they avoid the sterility of prepared scripts. Athletes are not trained speakers and with a script they would sound fake. Loosened up by a skillful interviewer, they choose their own words and it's a good bet many young people are more apt to listen to what they have to say than to their parents or other traditional mentors. Six hundred rock radio stations are already beaming out the word.

Here is one splendid opportunity for concerned parents to bring to their communities a tested idea. If you want some spots for your local station, write to Rock Project, 1111 Kearney Avenue, San Francisco, California 94133.

Planned Parenthood has also found new ways to reach youth. Its Dayton, Ohio, chapter seems to have scored a hit with a radio talk show, "Loving Carefully," a series of 5-minute spots focused on such topics as teen sex and pregnancy, sex education, parenting, and the male role in family planning. Mary Beth Moore of Planned Parenthood made a test appearance on one of Dayton's regular talk shows, which included an audience and a moderator known to be somewhat negative on contraception and family planning. Feedback from call-ins showed that what created most listener interest was Planned Parenthood's teen services given without parental consent and with a promise of complete confidentiality. On the basis of this knowledge, Moore was able to set up a program which dramatically increased the number of youngsters applying to Planned Parenthood, most of whom said they had heard the show. And so cleverly geared to youth was the show presented that calls coming into the station made it clear that public opinion was shifting on birth control issues.

   "Loving Carefully" is an interesting success, for radio stations are required by the FCC to donate part of their air time to public-service broadcasting. Though competition for this time is stiff, a good campaign inspired by parents can bring discussion of teen sexuality into your local station.

   If you want to reach teens through the media, communications experts at both Planned Parenthood and Population Institute warn that you should couch your message in their language and in the medium to which they are most frequently exposed. You would also do well to develop a pipeline of communication with key staff people at your selected station or publication. Avoid moralizing, specialists caution, and present an easy-to-use package, professional material, and interesting concepts for a talk show. Repetition, remember, instructs. Don't fear that making a point will turn off listeners.

> *"My friend has a problem*
> *I told her she should*
> *Talk in private with a friend*
> *At Planned Parenthood."*

Planned Parenthood in Ohio is hitting the airwaves with this jingle set to country rock and aired on rock stations. The spot brought 500 more teens in for sexual consultation than in any quarter ever before. It created such an influx that teen clinics had to be scheduled and a teen hot line set up from 9 P.M. to midnight, seven days a week. The flood of callers seems to show that, properly approached, teens will seek help.

Once having gotten them into the clinic, Planned Parenthood showed them films on adolescent sexuality as part of the counseling. But the Dayton branch reaffirmed the tested theory that one of the best ways to reach the young people flocking in was by a post-film rap session. The adolescents identified with the sexual problems in the film and could relate to a discussion which did not pin such trouble personally on them. The rap sessions were very important for, without guidance, any films the young people had seen were open to misinterpretation. One young girl, for example, watched a film evaluation of various contraceptive methods which made it clear that douching was a frail defense against pregnancy. In the subsequent rap session she raised her hand to inquire how soon after intercourse she should douche.

The Planned Parenthood staff is especially pleased to find that the rap session gave them an opportunity to "desensitize" the youngsters so that they felt able to talk about subjects which they had previously avoided. A skillful leader of such sessions can move well beyond the original point.

In New York City, the teens themselves are taking the initiative in finding new techniques for reaching their peers. Fourteen teenagers have organized a series of fast-paced improvisational skits working through problems concerned with sex and unwanted pregnancy and, as part of the Family Life Theatre, a brainchild of the Family Life Division of the ob/gyn department of New York Medical College, are reaching teens not usually responsive to such overtures.

The show is written by the kids themselves, who are certainly best able to judge what will hit home. They call it "Inside Out" and are showing it to everybody from ministerial groups to sixth-graders just starting out in the bewildering world of sex. The program, under the direction of Dr. Maria Boria, has even played an Off-Off-Broadway theater. After the show, the actors stay in costume and invite the audience to talk over what they have seen. The response has been called electrifying.

Hot lines, a concept only a little more than 10 years old, have proved again and again that their anonymity and immediacy make them valuable tools in the campaign against too-early pregnancy. Carefully monitored by a professional staff and a trained volunteer group, they give straight facts and nonthreatening communication to the many teenagers who have been turned off by the formality of clinics and the gap between them and the professional personnel.

Odd questions filter through the wire from the teenagers who represent 85 percent of the calls. Poured into the anonymous ear are all the fears and confusion that beset the minds of adolescents suffering through a difficult period. "How long is the average penis?" is a common question. "What can I do to make mine bigger?" "My breasts aren't big enough. Please help me."

What all this means basically is "Am I normal?" Adolescents are frequently dissatisfied with their bodies, and this may be one reason they don't get to clinics as often as they should. A trained hot-line volunteer operator can not only reassure such youngsters but refer them to agencies able to help them with problems which the seemingly odd questions only mask.

Dr. Murray Kappelman was associated with a hot line in Baltimore into which 38,000 calls poured, 50 percent of them cries for help about sexual matters. "These calls," says Dr. Kappelman, "strongly suggest that too many teenagers are not able to reach out to their parents or friends for help with their sexual crises. These adolescents must resort to the faceless confrontation . . . over the phone, usually very late at night."

Hot lines are being put into use by volunteer groups in many communities. If you think your town needs one, Jim McDonough, director of the Hotline Research Project, Center for Youth Development and Research, 325 Haecker Hall at the University of Minnesota, might have some advice.

One more avenue of approach to teens is moving up to supplement traditional centers like hospitals and family planning clinics. Groundbreaking new centers are moving away from a limited concern with pregnancy and contraception to positive emphasis on the human relationships in which they are involved.

The most widely imitated of all these is probably The Door, a Center of Alternatives, in New York City, mentioned earlier, a center which stresses the "whole person approach." The Door is a potpourri of youth services, physical and psychological, hidden away in an old warehouse in what social workers call a high-risk neighborhood. They don't mean that it is a high risk for mugging, but that teens in the area around 618 Avenue of the Americas where it is located are at high risk of becoming pregnant, or contracting venereal or other sex-related diseases.

You will recognize The Door by the number of young people standing around outside—smoking, talking, or just being. Teens flock to The Door because it is their place, offering them a sense of dignity, responsibility, and personal involvement they may not have known before.

Walking into The Door is like entering the tent where a three-ring circus is going on. In one corner a movie is being shown—*To Be a Man*—a film about the demands made on any normal boy growing up. Across the way a film slide show of a pelvic examination is being presented continuously so that no girl will be surprised when she seeks help in family planning at the health service.

Farther on is a rap session, an earnest group of young people discussing what girls think boys expect of them and what boys think girls expect. One girl is hotly arguing that to expect sex in exchange for a movie is a put-down. She is wearing a T-shirt inscribed "My Body Belongs to Me."

"We don't always want sex, but we like closeness,"

she says. "We expect some warmth, some caring, before we enter into a relationship which includes intercourse."

A boy in the audience remarks that he thinks all girls expect boys to perform sex satisfactorily and this bothers boys.

So it goes. Out in the open are questions that have bothered adolescents for years, getting a good shake-out laced with straight information by a skilled, often volunteer, counselor.

They come to The Door for everything from learning yoga to finding out if they are pregnant. They can get nearly anything here: free medical and gynecological services, nutrition counseling, psychiatric help, poetry seminars, theater, music, dance, and pottery making. The program will serve anyone between the age of 10 and 21, though most are 15 to 18. Fifty percent ask for family planning services.

The Door began as the dream of a group of dedicated volunteers and operated without any funding for several months after it opened in 1972. Now it is enormously successful and has imitators in urban America and as far away as Mexico. Its funds now come from federal and state governments, and voluntary contributions.

Rural parents worried that their adolescents have no access to such opportunities can take heart. The Montachusett Opportunity Council Family Planning and Health Center is just one example, this one in Massachusetts, of programs working to bring sex education to rural youth. *Teen Times,* the official magazine of the Future Homemakers of America, devoted an entire issue to teenage parenting recently, and the 4-H clubs have been offering sex education for some time. Rural communities can also send representatives to national conferences such as that of the National Youth Workers recently held at Georgetown University in Washington, D.C. Operating on the circuit system in which rural communities take turns sending representatives to city conferences, families living in less populated areas can have the benefit of expert advice on sex-related problems. Parents desiring to participate can write to the Population Institute Information Service.

For those outside the reach of preventive information, videotapes of rap sessions have turned out to be extremely useful. The East Oakland Planned Parenthood Unit has one presentation, aimed especially at male adolescents, which focuses on young males rapping in local hangouts. Showings of the tape at the Oakland Planned Parenthood clinic—followed by discussion—has attracted much interest. Single copies only of the tape are available free from the Family Planner (see Resource Guide).

An interesting new development in the area of giving more recognition to male responsibility in teenage pregnancy is a clinic set up especially for men. Details on how to set one up in your community are available from the Men's Reproductive Health Clinic (see Resource Guide). The new focus on the male is also evident in a Long Island radio program called "Tune In," run by two male high-school juniors in Great Neck who designed a discussion program concerning teenage views on sex matters. It is being aired on Long Island's biggest FM rock station.

I am encouraged to find how many cities are attempting to reach their teenagers in brand-new ways. Many are working together with representatives from the Population Institute assigned to their location, so that the new is tempered with the experience from established programs for youth.

A significant focus of the Population Institute is encouraging youth-serving organizations to further develop sex education in their programs. Des Moines, Seattle, and Cleveland have been training leaders in pilot programs along this line. The Sex Attitude and Knowledge Survey, referred to earlier and reproduced in part in the Resource Guide, is part of this effort. The Institute has been very successful in coordinating sex education courses for the youth program leaders of such organizations as the Salvation Army, the Boys Club of America, the Red Cross, and several churches of different denominations. At the initial study groups for organization leaders, 110 participants represented 47 concerned agencies.

Each has developed programs suited to its local interests. Seattle, for example, has decided to invite the mothers of the younger brothers to a meeting of Big Brothers led by a specialist on sex education. This is a way of giving little brothers the benefit of explanations of pitfalls older boys have encountered and at the same time helping mothers to become better sex educators. In Des Moines, Presbyterian churches have joined to put together an appropriate sex education curriculum for their youth. In Cleveland, several Boards of Directors of youth-serving agencies and churches are considering ways of integrating human sexuality aspects into ongoing programs that will be attractive to their youth membership

No longer are parents working alone, in a vacuum. A new spirit of cooperation between parents and various pertinent organizations may well make a difference in the number of unwanted babies born to teenagers.

12

Examining
Values:
The Essential
Ingredient

Masters and Johnson, those well-known investigators of human sexuality, told a large TV audience not long ago that considering the biological aspects of sex is not enough.

"Sexual intercourse," they said, "is not just a skill to be mastered, an activity to exercise the body, or a game to be played . . . To reduce sex to a physical exchange is to strip it of richness and subtlety and . . . ultimately means robbing it of all emotional value."

Once more I want to stress the importance of sex education, both formal and in the home. But reproductive information alone, while it may touch on the emotional side of human sexuality, cannot provide the kind of values that are the basis of a healthy, full sex life. We will shortchange our children if we do not give them something more. Ideally, values should have been absorbed through the atmosphere in the home from the cradle on, for building sound values through good human relations is a lifelong process.

All of us long for closeness with others, warm relations with someone who loves us. The need is built into us before we are born. Dr. Sarrel of Yale says that his work in a recent project concerning adults complaining of sexual problems revealed that 18 percent turned out to have spent long periods of childhood in isolation because of a life-threatening disease. They missed the intimate mother-child bonding, the touching that every infant comes into this world needing.

All of us long for closeness, but it takes us some time to learn to want to give it to others. The child is born narcissistic, intent on self-gratification. Some adults never leave this stage of development. Family attitudes go far in influencing loving responses. If we want to teach our children how to reach beyond themselves, we must begin while they are still impressionable. The best legacy we can leave them is the capability for making responsible decisions about themselves and others. This, of course, includes their sexual relationships.

A friend of mine, awaiting the arrival of a plane from Boston bringing her son home from a New England boarding school, once found herself sitting next to another woman who was there for the same reason. Comparing notes over their coffee, they discovered that both had recently found their sons' demeanor remote and self-interested. Both boys, they discovered, were mouthing jargon about "value judgments" and self-determination, all the while running roughshod over the sensibilities of others.

The woman took a sip of her coffee and put the cup down in its saucer.

"In the end," she said, "what it comes down to is being decent to the people around you."

She was right. Yet we must try to remember that the very nature of adolescence—this period in a human life cycle when the young individual is separating from family dependency, perhaps painfully, perhaps peacefully—is a time when it is difficult to avoid hurting parents. Consideration for others, that most desirable of all human qualities, is typically lacking at this age.

Can moral, like intellectual, development be nurtured in the growing child?

Dr. Lawrence Kohlberg, a leading Harvard psychologist, says it can. Methods derived from his theories about the growth of moral reasoning are now being utilized in classrooms across the country from the public schools of Tacoma, Washington, to the old-line private schools of New England. Kohlberg says his methods do not teach values but rather develop a decision-making ability which will be useful in solving moral problems.

He points out that up until the age of 7, our children are directed by fear of punishment. Pre-adolescents, he says, respond to the "morality of the marketplace," a reward for proper behavior shaping their acts. A somewhat older adolescent may excuse himself for bad behavior by saying that he meant well. Still later in life, law and order take precedence over personal inclination and desire to conform. Adults, many of whom never grow out of this stage, obey the law because they know they will be punished if they don't.

A highly mature stage of development involves being able to recognize that proper behavior is based on the social contract, from which the rights of individuals follow. Only 1 in 5 Americans ever reaches this level of maturity, says Kohlberg. Adults in this stage obey the law because they know it is the only viable means of maintaining order for all.

The highest level of moral reasoning is one based on universal principles involving justice, equality, reciprocity, and other ethical considerations. The Golden Rule is an example of this kind of principle.

Once armed with the decision-making ability, where do adolescents gain specific values? I believe that we parents, as the primary sex educators, initiate these values in the home. I do not think we can leave this to someone else to do for us. It is our business to give young people a sense of self-respect. I believe we must also teach them to respect their bodies. Children should learn this in the home and, as they grow, they can apply it to situations outside. This means being free to say no to sex they don't want. Only then will they truly value themselves as others will value them.

From this foundation of self-respect will grow the corollary that they must also respect others. This adds a sense of compassion to the principle of justice. We must build in our children a sense of obligation, both to themselves and others.

It is a lifelong process, this building of a sense of responsibility and decency. But it is the basis for a rich, rewarding life which sex will make more joyous and infinitely more pleasurable.

When children have learned that they must not hurt the people whose lives they touch, they will be ready to extend this concern to people they do not know. They will be on the road to becoming non-exploitive, caring

people who are mature enough to think beyond themselves, outward to humanity in the abstract, honoring, as
Kohlberg suggests the best of us may, the social contract.
And they will then have another good reason for the
proper use of contraception beyond protecting their own
options and their own futures—contributing to the good
of society by timing and limiting reproduction.

Throughout the learning process, parents can play
a vital role by supporting the adolescent's higher values
while pointing out how irresponsible sexual activities may
hinder the young person's ability to realize his life goals.

Possibly we tend to underestimate our young people. The
goals and values of teenagers, as revealed by the research
findings in the 1978 Youth Values Project, are startling.
When asked to rate 17 goals as "very important," "somewhat important," or "not important," both males and
females, regardless of race and socioeconomic status,
came up with *very future-oriented, serious, and responsible goals.*

The top four goal/values in order were:
1. getting a job I enjoy
2. preparing for my future
3. making it on my own
4. getting good grades

Having sex was thirteenth on the girls' list, with 27 percent ranking it "very important," and eighth on the boys'
list, with 55 percent rating it "very important."

A continuing trend toward accepting traditional
values is revealed in a 1979 survey of 21,000 achievers
drawn from student leaders listed in *Who's Who Among
American High School Students.* Seventy percent said
they had never had sexual intercourse and 60 percent

said they wanted to be virgins when married. Interestingly enough, the young people did not feel willing to impose their standards on others.

All this may offer an important clue to understanding normal adolescent aspirations that may be overlooked. Information without values is not enough. While even the most mature and well-directed adolescent will benefit from education about healthy human sexuality, a parent or counselor can add a new dimension by reinforcing the young person's own aspirations and primary values. Apparently many of our teenagers are keeping their options open, have constructive plans for the future, and—with a little help from us—will find their way along their chosen path.

Resource Guide

Books for parents and others working with adolescents

On Human Sexuality

Adolescent Sexuality in a Changing American Society, Catherine S. Chilman, U.S. Department of Health, Education and Welfare, #79-1426, 1979. An exhaustive summary of current research with annotated bibliography.

Adolescent Sexuality and Teenage Pregnancy, Karen Stewart Robb, Carolina Population Center, North Carolina, 1976.

Creative Approach to Sex Education and Counseling, 2d Ed., Patricia Schiller, M.A., J.D., Follett-Association Press, Chicago, Illinois.

Dealing With Questions About Sex, Arlene Uslander and Caroline Weiss, Learning Handbooks, 1975; $3.50 paper. Useful for counselors and modern parents.

Did the Sun Shine Before You Were Born? Sol Gordon and Judith Gordon, Ed-U Press, 1977; $2.95 paper. This is a book parents can read to their children. It is well illustrated. (Ages 4-9.)

Human Sexuality: New Directions in American Catholic Thought, prepared by the Catholic Theological Society of America, Paulist Press, 1977.

I Want to Keep My Baby! Joanna Lee, Signet Books, New American Library, 1977. A moving story of a thirteen-year-old girl who makes every effort to provide for the baby she loves. The touching story reveals the insurmountable odds against which teenagers in the younger age brackets struggle.

Learning About Sex: A Contemporary Guide for Young Adults, Gary F. Kelly, Barron's Educational Services, 1977; $3.50 paper. Includes innovative exercises for helping young people communicate about sex.

Love and Sex In Plain Language (Revised Edition), Eric Johnson, Bantam Books, Inc., 1974; $1.50 paper. This book, written frankly and plainly for teens, strengthens their values in caring, responsibility, and respect of self and others. It also gives basic information on a broad range of topics about human sexuality.

Only Human, Marion Howard, The Seabury Press, 1975. Pregnancy and the first years of young parenthood are described warmly and informatively in the story of the lives of three couples as they assume responsibility as parents.

Sex and the American Teenager, Murray M. Kappelman, M.D., Reader's Digest Press, 1977. This is a splendid book for parents, professional workers, and others who meet adolescents. They can take a sensitive look at adolescent sexuality through the eyes of a wise pediatrician who does not neglect the mental health of the parents and adolescents whose lives he touches.

Sex and Birth Control: A Guide for the Young, E. James Lieberman and Ellen Peck, Schocken Books, Inc., 1975; $2.45 paper. Parents may wish to share this book with young people who are facing dilemmas in building sexual values.

The Sexual Adolescent, Sol Gordon and Peter Scales, Duxbury Press, 1978. An easily read book based on solid research and the authors' skills in communicating.

Teach Us What We Want to Know, Ruth Byler, Gertrude Lewis, and Ruth Totman, Mental Health Materials Center, 1969; $3.00. Referred to in the text as a basic classic for counselors and parents.

"Where Did I Come From?" Peter Mayle, Lyle Stuart, Inc., 1973; $7.95. A long-popular book. Use with children has shown it to be precisely what they want and need. (Ages 4-9)

Your Child and Sex: A Guide for Parents, Wardell Pomeroy, Dell Publishing Co., Inc., 1976; $1.50 paper. A comprehensive book which moves from providing a better understanding of parents' own sexuality to clear discussions of sex from the youngest to post-adolescent age levels.

On Values

Adolescent Sexuality—e/sa forum-39, April 1978. Reprints available from *engage/social action,* 100 Maryland Avenue, N.E., Washington, D.C. 20002. (Order No. E-2039). 40ᶜ each; 10-99 copies, 35ᶜ each; 100 or more, 30ᶜ each. A stimulating collection of articles stressing the moral dimensions of this social concern from a broad range of contributors including the United Methodist Virginia Conference, the *Washington Post,* and others.

Helping Your Child Learn Right From Wrong: A Guide to Values Clarification, Sidney B. Simon, M.D., and Sally Wendkos Olds, McGraw-Hill, 1977; $2.95 paper. A basic text including innovative exercises for all ages and a broad range of value decisions, including sex.

Sex and Youth: A Symposium, Reprinted from *Top of The News* (Winter 1978). Available at a single-copy price of $1.75 from the Order Department, American Library Association, 50 E. Huron Street, Chicago, Illinois 60611. Outstanding specialists from a variety of fields discuss human sexuality and adolescent moral development, and place emphasis on the role of public libraries—especially the courage and wisdom of their staff—to help improve sexual knowledge among young people.

Values in Sexuality: A New Approach to Sex Educa-

tion, Eleanor S. Morrison & Mila Underhill Price, Hart Publishing co., Inc., 1974; $4.95 paper. This book recognizes a diversity in attitudes, feelings, and actions in the area of sexuality. It introduces specific strategies for including feelings about sexual issues as well as fundamental knowledge, and is widely used among modern sex educators.

Your Child's Self-Esteem, Dorothy Biggs, Dolphin Book, Doubleday & Co., 1975. A guide to treating teenagers with apathetic, unexamined lives who substitute irresponsible sexual activity for lack of more positive goals.

On Community Responsibility

Adolescent Fertility, The Proceedings of an International Conference, edited by Donald J. Bogue, Community and Family Study Center, University of Chicago, 1977. The proceedings of this landmark conference are a must for policy makers and program planners.

Children Having Children, Dawn Jax Belleau, The Sheboygan Press Charitable Foundation, 632 Center Avenue, Sheboygan, Wisconsin 53081, January 1978. A lively collection of seven news articles from the *Sheboygan Press,* this booklet stirs the community to face up to facts about teenage pregnancy. Especially recommended is the final chapter, "Learning to Say 'No.' "

Community Family Life Education Programs for Parents—A Training Manual for Organizers, Institute For Family Research and Education, 760 Ostrom Avenue, Syracuse, New York 13210. This volume is an invaluable training manual for parents or others organizing community family life education programs for parents.

School-Age Mothers: Problems, Programs and Policy, Lorraine V. Klerman and James F. Jekel, Shoestring Press, 1973; $6.00. A thoughtful review based on in-depth studies of the needs of pregnant girls. Useful in determining local goals.

Sex Counseling by Telephone, Preterm Institute, Schenkman Publishing Company, 1976. A book for groups interested in setting up community counseling through a hotline program.

Pamphlets

Government Publications

"Man of Today—The Man Who Cares," for sale by the Superintendent of Documents, U.S. Government Printing Office, Washington, D.C. 20402, 35¢ each, stock no. 017-031-00009-1. Published by the U.S. Department of Health, Education and Welfare, Public Health Service, Health Services Administration, Bureau of Community Health Services, Rockville, Maryland 20852. A sensitive treatment of today's male with an emphasis on interdependence with women rather than domination or control.

"Teenage Pregnancy—Everybody's Problem," for sale by the Superintendent of Documents, U.S. Government Printing Office, Washington, D.C. 20402, stock no. 017-026-00063-1. Published by the U.S. Department of Health, Education and Welfare, Public Health Service, Health Services Administration.

Other Publications

"Am I Parent Material?" A useful checklist for determining whether or not you should become a parent. Write to: National Alliance for Optional Parenthood, 3 North Liberty Street, Baltimore, Maryland 21201.

"Be Good to Your Baby Before It Is Born," National Foundation-March of Dimes, Box 2000, White Plains, New York 10602. 1973.

Planned Parenthood Publications

"Teen Sex: It's Okay to Say NO WAY," Planned Parenthood Federation of America, 810 Seventh Avenue, New York, New York 10019; Single copy 25¢; 100 for $15; 1,000 for $100.

"Parents Are the Facts of Life," Lee Minto, Planned Parenthood of Seattle/King County, 2211 E. Madison, Seattle, Washington 98112.

"Modern Methods of Birth Control," Planned Parenthood Federation of America, 810 Seventh Avenue, New York, New York 10019.

"How to talk to your teenagers about something that's not easy to talk about. Facts about the Facts of Life," Planned Parenthood Federation of America, 810 Seventh Avenue, New York, New York 10019. Single copy 25^c; 100 copies $12.00.

"Decisions . . . About Sex," Carol Craig, Planned Parenthood of Westchester, Inc., 149 Grand Street, White Plains, New York 10601.

"Assistance for the Sexually Active Female," Takey Crist, M.D., Youth and Student Affairs, Planned Parenthood Federation of America, 810 Seventh Avenue, New York, New York 10019.

"Sex Education at Home—A Guide for Parents," The Community Sex Education Center of Planned Parenthood Center of Syracuse, Inc., 1120 East Genesee Street, Syracuse, New York 13210, 1974.

Public Affairs Publications—Available from Public Affairs Pamphlets, 381 Park Avenue South, New York, New York 10016. Single pamphlets are $.50 each; larger quantities cost less.

"How to Tell Your Child About Sex"

"The Very New Baby: The First Days of Life"

"Talking to Pre-Teenagers About Sex"

"Sex Education: The Parents' Role"

"Preparing Tomorrow's Parents"

Student Publications—For older teens, written by student committees on sexuality.

"Elephants and Butterflies . . . and Contraceptives," R. Mier, D. Rollins. T. Blush, and T. Crist, 1975. Order from: C.C. Visual Aids, 200 Memorial Drive, Jacksonville, North Carolina 28540.

"Sex In a Plain Brown Wrapper," The Student Committee on Sexuality at Syracuse University, published in cooperation with the Student Health Service and the Institute for Family Research and Education.

The Student Guide to Sex On Campus, Student Committee on Human Sexuality, Yale University. Signet Book, New American Library, 1971.

Periodical Articles

A Special Issue on Teenage Pregnancy, *Family Planning Perspectives,* 10:4, 1978. Alan Guttmacher Institute, 515 Madison Avenue, New York, New York 10022.

"Early Motherhood: Ignorance or Bliss?" Harriet B. Presser, *Family Planning Perspectives,* 6:8, 1974.

"Sexual and Contraceptive Experiences of Young Unmarried Women in the United States, 1976 and 1977," M. Zelnik and J. Kantner, *Family Planning Perspectives,* 9:55, 1977.

"Teenagers: Fertility Control Behavior and Attitudes Before and After Abortion, Childbearing, or Negative Pregnancy Test," J.R. Evans, G. Selstad, W.H. Welcher, *Family Planning Perspectives,* 8:192, 1976.

"The Teenager Sexual Revolution and the Myth of an Abstinent Past," Phillips Cutright, *Family Planning Perspectives,* 4:1, 1972.

"A Supportive Service to Single Mothers and Their Children," Donna Tubach Heger, *Children Today,* September/October 1977, p. 3. Children's Bureau, DHEW Pub. No. (OHDS) 77-30014.

"The School Counselor in Sex Education," John J. Pietrofesa, *Personnel and Guidance Journal,* March 1976. Additional copies available from Youth and Student Affairs, Planned Parenthood Federation of America, 810 Seventh Avenue, New York, New York 10019.

"Adolescent Pregnancy and Childbearing—Growing Concerns for Americans," Wendy H. Baldwin, *Population Bulletin,* Vol. 31, No. 2, Population Reference Bureau, Inc.

Washington, D.C., 1976. This 36-page booklet is available, prepaid, from the Population Reference Bureau, P.O. Box 35012, Washington, D.C. 20013, for $1.00.

The Child, The Family and Responsible Parenthood (1978) has been produced for the International Year of the Child by the International Planned Parenthood Federation's Information Department. This package includes a paper which documents the relationship of family planning to the health, development, and welfare of the child, the mother, and the family; the IPPF policy statement for IYC; leaflets on issues such as adolescent fertility; charts, audiovisual aids and resource lists; and finally, a guide on how to adopt the package for local use. Available at no cost from IPPF Central Office, 18-20 Lower Regent Street, London SW1Y 4PW, England. Issued in English, French, and Spanish.

Eleven Million Teenagers: What Can Be Done about the Epidemic of Adolescent Pregnancies in the United States, Planned Parenthood Federation of America, 810 Seventh Avenue, New York, New York 10019. Single copy price $2.50.

Exploring Childhood: Program Overview and Catalog of Materials, Education Development Center, EDC School and Society Programs, Newton, Massachusetts, 1976. *Exploring Childhood* is a program in which high-school and junior-high-school students work with young children while learning about human development and their own identity. For a complete description of materials, including ordering information, write for a free catalog: Exploring Childhood, Education Development Center, School and Society Programs, 55 Chapel Street, Newton, Massachusetts 02160.

International Clearinghouse on Adolescent Fertility, The Population Institute, 110 Maryland Avenue, N.E., Washington, D.C. 20002. This clearinghouse will provide materials, program descriptions, research findings, and information about funding. Tel.: (202) 544-3300.

The Rights of Young People, Alan Sussman. Send $1.75 to Avon Books Mail Order Department, 250 West 55th

Street, New York, New York 10019, for this handbook by the American Civil Liberties Union on the rights of minors. It is a documented guide written in a question-and-answer format about medical care, contraception, abortion, and pregnancy.

School-Age Pregnancy and Parenthood in the United States, Lucy Eddinger and Janet Forbush, National Alliance Concerned With School-Age Parents, Washington, D.C., 1977. This is a report prepared by the National Alliance Concerned With School-Age Parents and is available from them, 7315 Wisconsin Avenue, Suite 211-W, Washington, D.C. 20014, for $5.00 per copy.

Men's Reproductive Health Clinic, Health Center #4, 1490 Mason Street, San Francisco, California 94133. Provides educational material especially beamed toward the interests of men.

Sex Information and Education Council of the U.S., Inc. Report, November 1978. *Human Sexuality: Books for Everyone.* This is a general and essential bibliography for anyone interested in sound information about human sexuality. It is especially useful for parents, young people, and those who work with them. Single copies of the bibliography are available from SIECUS on receipt of 25¢ and a stamped, self-addressed, legal-size envelope. Send to Sex Information and Education Council of the U.S. (SIECUS), 84 Fifth Avenue, New York, New York 10011.

Teenage Pregnancy: A Major Problem for Minors, prepared by Cynthia P. Green and Susan J. Lowe, Zero Population Growth, Inc. Copies may be obtained from Zero Population Growth, 1346 Connecticut Avenue, N.W., Washington, D.C. 20036. Single copies free; 2-49 copies 6¢ each; 50-199, 5¢ each; 200-499, 4¢ each; 500 or more, 3.5¢ each.

Teenage Pregnancy: A New Beginning, Linda Barr & Catherine Monserrat, 1978. This compilation was written by professionals with contributions by pregnant teenagers in a special school. It was prepared to help adolescents learn about themselves and their baby and is also full of useful information for parents who wish to be supportive during pregnancy, delivery, and early parenthood. Well illustrated. It is sold and distributed by New Futures, Inc., 110 Broadway, N.E., Albuquerque, New Mexico 87102.

The Youth Values Project, Susan Ross, Project Director. Available from The Population Institute, 110 Maryland Avenue. N.E., Washington, D.C. 20002. An inquiry, coordinated by teenagers themselves, into the attitudes, values, and experiences of teenagers in New York City regarding sex, contraception, and their life goals.

Films

"Guess Who's Pregnant?" Available from WTTW/Channel 11, Chicago Public Television, 5400 North St. Louis Avenue, Chicago, Illinois 60625, Tel: (312) 583-5000. A powerful documentary focusing on the personal tragedy of teenage motherhood and its negative impact on society. It examines the question of what parents, community leaders, educators, governments, and social agencies are doing about it.

"Children Raising Children." Available from the Children's Home Society, Como Street, St. Paul, Minnesota.

"Are You Ready For Sex?" A good springboard for discussion about whether or not to have an intimate relationship without including sex. Available from Perennial Education, Inc., 1825 Willow Road, P.O. Box 236, Northfield, Illinois 60093, Tel.: (312) 446-4153. 24 min., color, rent $30; purchase $300.

"Sex, Feelings, and Values." A group of films to trigger discussion based on 8–15 minutes of teenage, candid exploration of the following topics:

Sex Mis-Education
Sex Fears
Sex Morals
Early Homosexual Fears
Sex Games
Parents' Voices

For details, write to The Little Red Film House, 119 South Kilkea Drive, Los Angeles, California 90048.

Guidance Associates, 757 Third Avenue, New York, New York 10017, Tel: (212) 754-3700, offers a series of eight film strips and audio cassettes on the topic of Parenting:

Program #1—"Preparing for Parenthood"
Program #2—"Pregnancy"
Program #3—"Preparing for Birth"
Program #4—"Birth"
Program #5—"Adjusting to the New Baby"
Program #6—"Health Care for Mother and child"
Program #7—"Child Development"
Program #8—"The Parent as Teacher"

"Young, Single and Pregnant." A documentary film in which teenagers consider four different solutions to their pregnancies: adoption, abortion, marriage, and single parenthood. Available from Perennial Foundation, Inc., 1825 Willow Road, P.O. Box 236, Northfield, Illinois 60093, Tel.: (312) 446-4153.

Family Planner, Syntex Laboratories, 3401 Hillview Avenue, Palo Alto, California 94304. Supplies free of charge a newsletter and tapes on sex education subjects.

For a list of some of the best film and video cassette resources, write to Perennial Foundation, Inc., 1825 Willow Road, P.O. Box 236, Northfield, Illinois 60093, Tel: (312) 446-4153.

Directories

Congress and Federal Agencies 1977-78, Directory for Child Advocates. Published by Coalition for Children and Youth, 1910 K Street, N.W., Washington, D.C. 20006. Tel.: (202) 785-4180.

For a directory of hot lines, write:
The Communication Company
1826 Fell Street
San Francisco CA 94117

Also, look under Social Services in the yellow pages of your telephone book.

Planned Parenthood Affiliates and Chapters. This listing includes Certified Affiliates and their Chapters. Available from Planned Parenthood Federation of America, Inc., 810 Seventh Avenue, New York, New York 10019. Seven out of ten people live in areas served by Planned Parenthood; check the white pages of your telephone book.

Organizations

The Alan Guttmacher Institute
515 Madison Avenue
New York, New York 10022

American Association of Sex Educators, Counselors, and
   Therapists (AASECT)
5010 Wisconsin Avenue
Washington, D.C. 20017

Carolina Population Center
Publications Office
123 West Franklin Street
Chapel Hill, North Carolina 27514

Catholic Alternatives
30 East 23d Street
New York, New York 10010

Child Welfare League of America
67 Irving Place
New York, New York 10003
Tel.: (212) 254-7410

Coalition for Children and Youth
1910 K Street, N.W.
Washington, D.C. 20002
Tel.: (202) 785-4180

Institute for Family Research and Education
760 Ostrom Avenue
Syracuse, New York 13210

The National Alliance Concerned with School-Age Parents
(NACSAP)
7315 Wisconsin Avenue, Suite 221-W
Washington, D.C. 20014

National Alliance for Optional Parenthood
3 North Liberty Street
Baltimore, Maryland 21201

National Institutes of Health
Behavioral Sciences Branch
National Institute of Child Health and Human Development
Rockville, Maryland 20852

Planned Parenthood Federation of America, Inc.
810 Seventh Avenue
New York, New York 10019

Population Crisis Committee
Suite 550
1120 19th Street, N.W.
Washington, D.C. 20036
Tel.: (202) 657-1833

The Population Institute
110 Maryland Avenue, N.E.
Washington, D.C. 20002
Tel.: (202) 544-3300

The Salvation Army
120 West 14th Street
New York, New York 10011
—The Salvation Army has a collection of Education for Parenthood curricula.

Sex Information and Education Council of the United States,
  Inc. (SIECUS)
84 Fifth Avenue, Suite 407
New York, New York 10011

United States Department of Health, Education and Welfare
Administration for Children, Youth and Families
Washington, D.C. 20025

State Policies on Public Funding of Abortions for Medicaid-Eligible Women (Courtesy The Alan Guttmacher Institute)

Voluntarily Paying for All or Most Abortions—9 states and Washington, D.C.

Alaska	Maryland	Oregon
Colorado	Michigan	Washington
Hawaii	New York	District of Columbia
	North Carolina	

Hyde Amendment-type Language—19 states

Alabama	Maine	Oklahoma
Arkansas	Mississippi	South Carolina
California**	Montana	Tennessee
Delaware	Nevada	Texas
Georgia	New Hampshire	Vermont
Idaho	Ohio	Wisconsin
Indiana		

Paying for Life, Rape and Incest Indicated-Abortions—5 states

Iowa*	Massachusetts*	New Mexico
Kansas	Minnesota	

Paying for Abortions to Save the Woman's Life Only—16 states

Connecticut	Nebraska	South Dakota
Florida	New Jersey*	Utah
Illinois**	North Dakota	Virginia*
Kentucky	Pennsylvania*	West Virginia*
Louisiana*	Rhode Island	Wyoming
Missouri**		

Paying for "medically indicated or necessary" or "health-indicated" abortions under court order.
**Paying for Hyde Amendment-type abortions under court order.*
Probable fetal deformity allowable abortion indication under Medicaid.

Selected material from "The Sex Attitude and Knowledge Survey" (Courtesy The Population Institute)

Survey prepared by:
James C. Petersen, Ph.D.; Lawrence A. Morris, Ph.D.
Behavior Associates
Tucson, Arizona 85701

Judith Senderowitz, MA, Executive Director; William Ryerson, M. Phil.,
Student and Youth Division
The Population Institute
110 Maryland Avenue NE, Washington D.C. 20002

Attitudes Toward Human Sexuality

	PRE					POST				
	STRONGLY AGREE				STRONGLY DISAGREE	STRONGLY AGREE				STRONGLY DISAGREE
	1	2	3	4	5	1	2	3	4	5
Adolescents should have the right to sex information even if their parents are opposed.										
The increase in premarital sexual intercourse is primarily related to the increase in sex education programs and efforts.										
Regardless of a person's age, contraceptive services and information should be made available.										
Abortion is wrong and should never be allowed.										
Abortion should be a woman's choice.										

Knowledge of Human Sexuality

	PRE			POST		
	I AGREE	I DO NOT AGREE	I DON'T KNOW	I AGREE	I DO NOT AGREE	I DON'T KNOW
Most profesionals and educators believe that masturbation in adolescence often leads to sexual dysfunction in later years.						
Anxiety over heterosexual experiences is a common factor leading to homosexulality in adolescence.						
Some homosexual behavior is a normal part of growing up.						
According to recent studies, only 25% of 15- to 19-year-old, unmarried women have had sexual intercourse.						
Between the ages of 15 to 19, about one out of every ten females becomes pregnant.						
A majority of high-school-aged girls who become pregnant go on to complete high school.						

Knowledge of Human Sexuality

	PRE			POST		
	I AGREE	I DO NOT AGREE	I DON'T KNOW	I AGREE	I DO NOT AGREE	I DON'T KNOW
The average age of a girl at first menstruation is 12½ years.						
More than half of all adolescent women having their first sexual intercourse use contraception.						
Since 1970, the birth rate for U.S. teenagers (aged 15-19) has increased sharply.						
Most teenagers seeking clinical birth control services do so before their first sexual intercourse experience or within 3 months following.						
In all states, teenagers can legally obtain contraceptives without parental consent.						
The condom is the only contraceptive which limits the spread of venereal disease.						
The two primary ways that a majority of teenagers learn about sexuality is through the media and their peers.						

Index   181

Index

A
Abdul-Jabbar, Kareem, 148
Abortion, 81-96 passim
  clinics, 85, 87-88, 90-92
  costs, 92
  procedures, 89-90
Adolescence, 35-38, 40-41
Adolescent Clinic, Roosevelt
  Hospital (New York City), 68
Adolescent Health Services and
  Pregnancy Prevention and
  Care Act, 129
Adolescent Pregnancy Program, 96
"Adolescent slouch," 31
Adoption, 76-80
Aid to Families with Dependent
  Children (AFDC), 75, 108-10
American Association of Sex
  Educators, Counselors and
  Therapists (AASECT), 29, 54
American Library Association, 123

B
Baby, expenses of, 110-11
"Baby-doll syndrome," 76
Baldwin, Wendy, 18
Barton, Clara, 148
Better Homes and Gardens
  (magazine), 22
Big Brothers, 156
Big Sisters, 111
Boria, Maria, 151
Boyd, Lauren, 119
Boys Club of America, 156
Breasts, growth of, 31-32

C
Cafritz Foundation, 135
Calderone, Mary, 35, 141
Califano, Joseph, 110
California Union of Primary Health
  Providers, 138-39
Campbell, Arthur, 16
Campfire Girls, 147
Carnegie Corporation, 24
Carrera, Michael, 141, 142
Cates, Willard, Jr., 89
Catholic Alternatives, 86-87
Catholic Charities Organization, 112
Center for Youth Development and
  Research, University of
  Minnesota, 44
Changing Trends, 50

Chelton, Mary K., 123-24
Chicago Planned Parenthood, 61
Child abuse, 18-19
Child Welfare League of America,
  Inc., 99, 107, 142, 143
Children's Bureau (HEW), 9
Chilman, Catherine, 37-38
Cleveland Foundation, 24
Coalition for Children and Youth,
  51, 131
Collins, Barbara-Rose, 115
Columbia University College of
  Physicians and Surgeons
  Center for Population and
  Family Health, 122
Colwell, Jean, 77
Community Council of Greater
  New York, 110
Community Family Life Education
  Programs for Parents (training
  manual), 52
Condoms, 32, 34
Contraception, 32, 91-92
Contraceptives, attitudes toward use
  of, 1-2
Cooper, Alice, 148
Crist, Takey, 84-85, 89, 90, 95
Crist Clinic for Women, 84
Cutright, Phillips, 47

D
Day care, 110
Delaware Adolescent Program,
  Inc. (DAPI), 101
Diaphragm, 32
D&C (dilation and curettage), 90
Divorce, 15-16
Donahue, Phil, 21
Door, The, a Center of Alternatives
  (New York City), 153-54
Drugs, 7-8
Duncan, Margaret, 116

E
Education, 104-5
Emory Grady Hospital Teen
  Services Program (Atlanta,
  Ga.), 44
Erikson, Erik, 113
Everly, Kathleen, 52
Exercise, 103

F
Fairfax County, Virginia, 117-20
Family Life Theatre, 151

Family Planner, 155
Family Service Society, 112
Federal Communications
    Commission (FCC), 126
FDA Bureau of Foods, 71
Florence Crittenton Program,
    98-99, 107
Forbush, Janet, 11
Forever (Blume), 124-25
Fox, Greer Litton, 10, 131
Future Homemakers of America,
    154

G
Gadpaille, Warren, 29
Gambino, Gina, 119
Gause, Ralph, 68
Gender identity, 26-27
George Mason Junior-Senior High
    School (Falls Church, Va.),
    120-22
Georgia Human Resources
    Department, 18
Girls Club of America, 147
Goldsmith, Gary, 57
Goldsmith, Sadja, 65
Gordon, Sol, 52
Guttmacher, Alan, Institute, 3, 13,
    114

H
Hamilton, Eleanor, 58
Harriman, Joan, 86-87
Hayfield High School (Fairfax
    County, Va.), 119, 122
*Helping Your Child Learn Right
    From Wrong* (Simon and
    Olds), 39
Hirsh, Michael, 3-8, 10
Homosexuality, 29-30
Hot lines, 151-52
Hotline Research Project, 152
*How to Talk to Your Teenagers
    About Something That's Not
    Easy to Talk About* (Planned
    Parenthood), 31
Howard, Marion, 44
"Human Sexuality: Books for
    Everyone" (SIECUS), 24
Hutcher, Francis, 49
Hyde Amendment, 93, 94

I
Illegitimacy, rate of, 11
"Inside Out" (play), 151

Institute for Family Research and
    Education (Syracuse, N.Y.), 52,
    58, 122-23
Intercourse, 32
IUD, 32

J
Jacobs, Elaine, 55
Johns Hopkins Center for School-
    Age Mothers and Their Infants,
    100-1
Johns Hopkins School of Public
    Health, 13
Johnson Foundation, 107
Jones, Margaret, 51, 147

K
Kantner, John, 13
Kappelman, Murray, 152
Kenniston, Kenneth, 22
Kentner, John, 110
Kirkpatrick, J. Stephen, 62-63
Kohlberg, Lawrence, 159-60, 161
Kolbye, Albert, 71
Konopka, Gisela, 44
Kushner, Irving, 130

L
Landers, Ann, 62
Law Center of the Student Press,
    119
Lesbianism, 33
Louisiana Family Planning Program,
    12
"Loving Carefully" (radio show),
    149
Lowe, Charles, 17
Lubin Finkel, David, 61-62
Lubin Finkel, Madelon, 61-62
Lynn, Loretta, 148

M
McCutcheon, Lawrence, 148
McDonough, Jim, 152
McKusick, Marjorie, 142
Male sexuality, 57-66 *passim*
    female attitudes toward, 59-60
MAN program (Rochester, N.Y.),
    64
"Man of Today—the Man Who
    Cares" (HEW), 64-65
Markowitz, Elysa, 103-4
Masters and Johnson, 157
Masturbation, 23-24, 29, 33
Maynard, Joyce, 124

Men's Reproductive Health Clinic, 155
Menses, 11, 18-19, 31
Menstruation, 30-32
Merrill Palmer Institute, 10
Montachusett Opportunity Council Family Planning and Health Center, 154
Moore, Mary Beth, 149
Morgenthau, Joan, 36
Movement to Restore Decency in Education, 116, 117

N
National Alliance Concerned with School-Age Parents, 11, 105
National Center of Child Advocacy, 145
National Center for Disease Control (Atlanta, Ga.), 18
National Center for Health Statistics, 11
National Conference of Catholic Bishops, 127
National Council of the Churches of Christ in the USA, 127
National Family Sex Education Week, 123, 124
National Institute of Child Health and Human Development, 133
National Institutes of Health, 16
National Institute of Mental Health, 145
National Organization of Non-Parents, 120
National Red Cross, 147-48, 156
National Youth Workers, 154-55
New York Charities Aid Association, 47
Nix, Lulu Mae, 101, 104
Nutrition, 102

O
Oettinger, Malcolm, 125-26
Office of Adolescent Pregnancy, 129
Office of Child Development, 145
Office of Education, 145
Otterbacker, John, 116

P
Parent Effectiveness Training, 39-40
Parenting programs, 145-47

Parents
  attitudes toward illegitimacy, 99-100
  relationship to teenagers, 5-8
  response toward new grandchild, 111-12
  response to teenage pregnancy, 10-11, 68-69, 72-76
  role in sex education, 21-41 *passim*, 43-55 *passim*
Parents Council of Washington, 50
Peer counseling, 133-43 *passim*
Perspectives (magazine), 13
Philliber, Susan, 122
Pills, birth control, 32
Pilpel, Harriet F., 129
Planned Parenthood, 49, 64, 70, 92, 149-50
Planned Parenthood v. Danforth, 83
Planned Parenthood of Metropolitan Washington, 135
Planned Parenthood of Southern Arizona, 62
Population Institute, 25, 47, 64, 134, 148, 149, 155, 156
Population Institute Information Service, 155
Pregnancy, 57, 67-80 *passim*
  exercise during, 103
  nutrition during, 102
  perils of for teenagers, 16-19
  reaction of parents to, 72-76
  reasons for among teenagers, 12-14
  smoking during, 102-3
  test for, 70-72
Premarital sex, 32
Preterm Institute (Boston, Mass.), 137-38
Project Girl, 147
Project on Human Sexual Development, 24, 30, 34, 49-50
Prostaglandins, 90
Puberty, 11, 35-36
  delayed, 27-28

R
Raspberry, William, 147
Religious institutions, role of in sex education, 127
Reluctant Regulators, The (Oettinger), 125
Roberts, Elizabeth M., 34

Rock Project, 148-49
Rockefeller, John D., III, 24,
   114-15
Ross, Susan, 48
Rubin, Isadore, 141
Ryerson, William, 134

S
St. Anne's Home for Unwed
   Mothers (Los Angeles, Cal.),
   16
Salt procedure, 90
Salvation Army, 99, 156
Sarrel, Philip, 25, 28, 44, 158
Scales, Peter, 58
Sex Attitude and Knowledge
   Survey, 25, 156
"Sex, Can It Teach Itself?" (TV
   show), 123
Sex Counseling by Telephone
   (Preterm Institute), 137
Sex Information Center
   (Washington, D.C.), 135-36
Sex Information and Education
   Council of the U.S. (SIECUS),
   24, 35
Sex at Yale, 141
Sexual Development Study, 33
Smoking, 102-3
Sorenson, R. C., 60
"Sports Project, The," 64
Student Coalition for Relevant Sex
   Education (New York City),
   139-40
Suction curettage, 89-90
Synagogue Council of America,
   127

T
Tatum, Mary Lee, 43, 120, 121-22
Teach Us What We Want to Know
   (Byler, Lewis, and Totman), 26
Teen Advocacy Project, 138-39
Teen Hotline, 87
Teen Scene (TV show), 4
Teen Times (magazine), 154
Teenage Pregnancy, Everybody's
   Problem (HEW), 45
"Teenage Sexual Revolution and
   the Myth of an Abstinent Past,
   The" (Cutright), 47

Television, influence of, 125-27
Temple Hospital Family Planning
   Center, 49
To Be a Man (film), 153
Tracey Education Center (Cerritos,
   Cal.), 105-6
"Tune In" (radio show), 155

U
United Methodist Church, 127
UN Population Conference
   (Bucharest, Rumania), 19

V
Values Clarification Training, 39
Values in Sexuality (Morrison and
   Price), 40
Venereal disease, 14

W
WEPR (Clemson, S.C.), 4
Wet dreams, 28-29
"What Is It?" 87
"What Your Teenage Daughter
   Wants to Tell You About
   Sex" (Hirsh), 3-8
Where Did I Come From? (Mayle),
   24
Who's Who Among American High
   School Students, 161-62
Winfield, Louise, 117-18, 122
"Wingspread" conference, 107, 108
Wise, Louise, Services (New York
   City), 107
Wolverton, E. Dollie, 146-47
World Health Organization, 20

Y
Yale Sexuality Program, 140-41
Yale University Student Health
   Center, 44
Youth Value Project, 47-48,
   54-55, 60, 161

Z
Zelnik, Melvin, 13, 110